TRANSFORM YOUR GARDEN
ON A Budget

How we keep our garden says a lot about us – what does yours say about you? Whatever outdoor space you have, it needn't be expensive nor hard work to turn into your dream retreat! In this brand-new title from the makers of Style at Home, we share our favourite garden transformations from the magazine, as well as inspirational ideas and fun projects to help your outdoor space channel the real you.

Whether your garden consists of patio, or a chaotic wilderness of trees and plants, we've got plenty of suggestions to tame nature and harness the power of plants to make your space sing! We'll also share our experts' advice on how to incorporate garden buildings into your space, what to plant in every corner of your garden, and what you can do to turn your garden into the ideal entertaining space.

CONTENTS

Inside...

116 Gardening calendar
Discover tasks, projects and maintenance for every month to keep your garden blooming

DESIGN ADVICE

6 WHAT'S YOUR STYLE?
Designing a theme for your garden can be tricky. We've put together a guide on our favourite planting styles to help you decide

10 DESIGN MASTERCLASS
Getting the perfect layout for your garden can be tricky. Garden designer Tabi Jackson Gee provides easy solutions for the most common problems

16 GARDEN DESIGN ON A BUDGET
Ten ideas to stretch your cash outdoors and maximise your plot's potential

24 ZONE YOUR OUTDOOR SPACE
Use clever zoning ideas in the garden to create a multifunctional space for the family

48 PERFECT PATIOS
Choose the right surface for your seating area with our easy guide to the best patio materials

68 CREATE THE PERFECT SHADY SPOT
Provide a sheltered area so you can enjoy your outdoor space whatever the weather

92 GET CREATIVE WITH PAINT
Give your outdoor space a facelift using striking paint treatments

GARDENING TIPS

38 LAWN CARE 101
Basic steps to look after your lawn, from mowing to sowing

76 THE BLUFFER'S GUIDE TO SOIL
Everything you need to know about your garden's planting medium

78 50 GREAT VALUE PLANTS FOR BUDGET GARDENING
A beautiful and productive garden needn't cost the earth, simply choose the right plants

110 365 DAYS OF COLOUR
Garden designer Tabi Jackson Gee shares the easy tricks garden designers use to get colour into gardens all year round

BUYERS' GUIDES

40 LAWN TOOLS
Everything you need to know about the kit to keep your lawn at its luscious best

38

48

58 OUTDOOR COOKING
Broaden your horizons with a barbecue or pizza oven

88 GARDEN STRUCTURES
How to build livability into your outdoor space

102 GARDEN HEATING
The warm heart of your garden glow-up

PROJECTS

32 GARDEN STORAGE SOLUTIONS
Tidy your outdoor space with easy repurposing and upcycling ideas

54 LAY YOUR OWN PATIO
Laying a stone patio yourself is cheaper than paying someone to install an expensive alternative and it only takes a couple of days!

62 OUTDOOR KITCHEN STORAGE
Organise your cooking kit with these inexpensive garden storage options and projects

70 MAKE AN OUTDOOR CHANDELIER
Bring a magical glow to evenings outdoors with this fabulous garden lighting idea that is super-simple to put together

10

24

4 | TRANSFORM YOUR GARDEN ON A BUDGET

CONTENTS

96 PAINT A TIERED HERB PLANTER
Revamp tired-looking timber with a bold paint treatment that will transform a plain planter into a unique and colourful piece

REAL TRANSFORMATIONS

20 'IT'S SO PRETTY IN FULL BLOOM'
Florist Deborah took a neglected back garden and turned it into a modern country space filled with flowers

34 GOING GREEN
Re-planning their garden in tandem with building a new extension helped Adam and Irenie create a flexible outdoor space for the family

44 'WE'RE HAPPY TO POTTER'
Hampered by a lack of green fingers, Susan and Henry hired a professional to turn their small garden into a low-maintenance outdoor room

64 WELL INCLINED
Judith and Michael made their garden more usable by dividing it into split-level spaces, each with its own look, feel and purpose

72 PLANT-FILLED HAVEN
Pauline has transformed a featureless space into an elegant, contemporary garden, complete with cutting patch, pond and seating

84 A FAMILY AFFAIR
With spaces for eating, socialising, alone time and hobbies, Tracey and Paul have created a garden specially designed to suit every member of their family

98 'WE NOW HAVE AN EXTRA ROOM'
Keen to transform her neglected garden, Mel created a low-maintenance outdoor space that's great for relaxing

106 DOWNTOWN OASIS
Owners Antony and Christopher have turned a traditional town garden into a tropical paradise

TRANSFORM YOUR GARDEN ON A BUDGET | 5

What's your STYLE?

Designing a theme for your garden can be tricky. We've put together a guide on our favourite planting styles to help you decide

Small space exotic
You don't need to have a huge garden to create an impactful tropical look – big leaves have greater impact. Cordyline and ferns are fine in containers. A passion flower will romp about with its roots growing in very little space.

GO EXOTIC!

Key plants for this look

Trachycarpus fortunei
With the classic exotic look, the Chusan palm is hardy in UK winters, even in snow! It provides height, drama and shade. It's slow-growing but reaches 15m eventually.

Dicksonia antarctica
This is like a big fern on a stem, with huge lacy leaves. Grow it in shade. It's semi-evergreen but needs protection from frost.

Canna
Cannas really ramp up the tropical vibe in your space, with colourful foliage and flowers in hot reds and oranges. With strong vertical accents, they'll flower all summer, but need winter protection.

Exotic gardens can make you feel like you're on holiday all year round! Lush, green spaces with dramatic foliage punctuated by vibrant colour, they're great for city gardens where higher temperatures protect plants from frost. Evergreens give fantastic winter presence. The secret? Choose plants hardy in winter that look exotic, like *Fatsia japonica*. You'll need to bring tender plants inside in winter.

HOW TO PLANT

✷ Choose tall evergreens with bold foliage like *Trachycarpus*, or *Eriobotrya* (loquat tree). Add drama with spiky feature plants like cordylines.

✷ Underplant with dense ground cover – evergreen ferns and grasses are perfect. In summer, *Crocosmia* 'Lucifer' provides swordlike leaves and sizzling colour.

✷ Add cannas and cactus-type dahlias, like 'Indian Summer'. Give them a sunny spot and protect in winter.

WHAT'S YOUR STYLE?

Small space cottage
If you've only a small patio, grow compact roses like 'Phyllis Bide' in a pot. For scent, honeysuckle 'Rhubarb and Custard' will also be happy in a container. Plant in old buckets or fruit crates – anything with patina is perfect.

QUAINT COTTAGE

Say 'cottage garden' and you picture roses and honeysuckle romping over a rustic arch, colourful herbaceous borders brimming with delphiniums and lupins, as well as veg, fruit and herbs. Cottage style looks great but can be high maintenance. Rock the cottage look by choosing reliable, long-flowering varieties. Colour scheme your borders to avoid a 'tutti-frutti' look – pinks and purples are classic cottage.

HOW TO PLANT
✴ Keep your layout simple, so planting can shine. Include evergreens for winter – cover an arch with ivy, topiary and shrubs like choisya.

✴ A fruit tree is a must-have, for spring blossom, autumn colour and fruit. Add flowering shrubs – lilac and peonies for early summer and hydrangeas to follow on.

✴ Combine flowering plants with herbs like rosemary and chives. Pop decorative veg like beetroot 'Bull's Blood' into the border too.

Key plants for this look

Roses
Roses are essential to this style. 'Munstead Wood' (dark red) or 'Gertrude Jekyll' (pink) are good. Grow climbing roses like 'Zephirine Drouhin' (pink) over an arch or up an apple tree.

Daisies
Daisies epitomise the cottage look. Aster 'Little Carlow' and 'Monch' flower from late summer till autumn.

Sweet peas
Sweet peas provide masses of colour and swoonsome scent for cutting, and are easily seed-grown. Plant in the ground or a pot, and tie in to a wigwam of pea sticks or a rusty tripod.

WORDS: GERALDINE SWEENEY. PHOTOS: ALAMY, GAP PHOTOS, MARIANNE MAJERUS

TRANSFORM YOUR GARDEN ON A BUDGET | 7

Small space urban

The urban contemporary look is perfect for compact gardens. Use simple, geometric containers with evergreen plants. Choose a sculptural focal point – a statue or plant. Max out your planting space with a stylish green wall.

Key plants for this look

Olea europaea
Olive trees provide a permanent silvery presence, working well in containers. They don't mind cold but hate getting their feet wet, so plant in well-drained soil in the sun.

Pleached hornbeam (Carpinus betulus)
These trees are like hedges on stilts and are good dividers in urban gardens. You can also pleach crabapple, beech, or lime.

Ophiopogon planiscapus 'Nigrescens'
This serves as stylish ground cover. Its black 'evergreen' leaves look good all year round in the ground or in containers. It's slow-growing and gradually spreads outwards.

MODERN URBAN

This style needs to look good all year round. Plants are usually in containers or raised beds with a minimalist look, using smooth materials, like chrome or stainless steel. They're planted in lines or groups, with much repetition of key shapes, like topiary in balls or cubes. Colour is muted – form is more important. Contemporary furniture and lighting create a stylish, uncluttered look.

HOW TO PLANT

✱ Choose sculptural evergreen plants that look good all year round, like yew or bay. Have fewer varieties but in greater numbers and repeat, repeat, repeat.

✱ Include a bold focal point – maybe a multi-stemmed birch or amelanchier, or cloud-pruned topiary. Uplight for extra impact.

✱ Ground cover can be low-growing plants or just pebbles. Finish the look with contemporary furniture and a well-chosen sculpture.

WHAT'S YOUR STYLE?

Small space wildlife
A small tree gives great value in a small space, providing blossom in spring, berries in June and autumn colour. Try compact buddleia 'Buzz' which grows to 1.2m. Sedum, the ice plant, gives long-lasting colour in containers or the ground.

WILDLIFE HAVEN

A wildlife garden is alive with birds flitting through the trees, bees and butterflies thrumming in the flowers, and hedgehogs in the long grass. To attract a wide variety of wildlife you'll need to include a range of mini habitats, such as ponds, meadows or woodland areas, and hibernation sites for insects and small mammals. Wildlife style needs to be natural but that doesn't mean it has to be untidy.

HOW TO PLANT
✻ Choose a variety of trees and shrubs – evergreens for cover and fruit trees for birds to nest and roost in.
✻ A pond will attract dragonflies and amphibians.
✻ Let your lawn grow long or make it into a meadow – naturalise bulbs for spring, or wildflower plug plants like poppies for summer. Include yellow rattle to kill grass roots so the wildflowers can flourish.

Key plants for this look

Viburnum opulus 'Compactum'
This shrub has bunches of red berries in autumn which birds love. Lacy white flowers in spring attract pollinators like hoverflies and early bees.

Buddleia davidii 'Royal Red'
This large shrub comes in a range of colours, but red is a butterfly favourite, they crowd the conical flowers in summer.

Centranthus ruber (Valerian)
Adored by butterflies, this perennial flowers almost non-stop from May to October. It needs a sunny spot and an exposed area and doesn't mind poor soil. It comes in red, mauve and white.

TRANSFORM YOUR GARDEN ON A BUDGET | 9

Design MASTERCLASS

Getting the perfect layout for your garden can be tricky. Garden designer Tabi Jackson Gee provides easy solutions for the most common problems

When it comes to gardens, there isn't a one-size-fits-all approach, which can be very daunting to a novice gardener! However, there are some practical steps you can take when designing your outdoor space – and these are the ones that I turn to when working with new clients.

From tiny gardens to awkward shapes, there are tried-and-tested ways to get the best possible result. Here, you'll find handy tips and planting ideas to help get you started. Good luck!

DESIGN MASTERCLASS

THE MULTIPURPOSE GARDEN

Play area and outdoor kitchen meets relaxing oasis: so many of us have gardens that have to fulfil myriad different roles, but how on earth do you fit all these in one modest plot?

The key is not to divide the space up too formally (who has room for all that anyway?) but instead to think about what times of day and year the garden will be used for what and lay it out from there. There are plenty of ways to make your garden truly multifunctional – while keeping everyone happy!

Style tips

1 If you need an area for kids to play, create walled spaces or raised beds for plants or choose hardy specimens that won't mind being hit by a football every now and again.

2 A grass lawn is good as it provides a soft place to play. Or try other mat-forming plants like creeping thyme (*Thymus serpyllum*) and mind-your-own-business (*Soleirolia soleirolii*).

3 Be mindful of storage – look out for clever seat, planter and storage combinations.

4 Think about the views you want. If you have children you will want to keep an eye on them – but also provide space for them to explore. Use low hedging or planted areas to create room for adventures.

5 Additionally, install living plants to create tunnels, teepees and hiding places. Water Willows (waterwillows.com) provide kits with handy step-by-step instructions.

3 of the best... PLANTS FOR A BUSY GARDEN

HYDRANGEA MACROPHYLLA 'AYESHA'
The blooms last for months, they're suited to both sun and shade, and they're low maintenance.

HEBE 'GREEN GLOBE'
A lovely shrub that is also delightfully compact and, with some gentle pruning, can be kept that way. Flowers in May and June.

SANTOLINA CHAMAECYPARISSUS
Also known as lavender cotton, add this delicious herb to soups and broths. Plant in a sunny spot.

TRANSFORM YOUR GARDEN ON A BUDGET

THE AWKWARDLY SHAPED GARDEN

Unless you live in a new build, it's not always possible to find a garden that's a regular shape. Long, thin, bulbous – gardens can feel unbalanced unless you use a design that either detracts from your odd bits, or makes the most of them.

Try imposing shapes on them or using focal points to detract the eye from unseemly corners. It's extremely achievable to bring some sense and order to your misshapen outdoor space.

3 of the best... SHADE-TOLERANT PLANTS

DIGITALIS PURPUREA
Foxgloves, as they're more commonly known, are brilliant plants for shade and will self-seed. They're also great for pollinators and flower from early summer.

DRYOPTERIS FILIX-MAS
Growing wild in many UK woodlands, this fern requires ample watering during its first summer. The fronds die back in winter, so fill the gaps with bulbs.

HOSTA FORTUNEI 'FRANCEE'
Purple flowers appear in late summer, and it'll thrive in a shaded planter. Snails and slugs love it, so best placed above ground level.

Style tips

1 If your garden has weird angles or an extra lump on the end of it, don't let that steer how you use it. Impose a rectangle, square or circle on it, in the form of a lawn or patio, and use that to shape the layout of your garden.

2 Side returns are often dark and uninspiring. A large mirror set above a statement planter with shade-tolerant ferns in containers will instantly banish the dingy corridor vibes.

3 Every modern garden should have room for compost – put it in a spot you don't have any other use for. It's a great way to reuse household green waste to help plants thrive.

4 If one part of your garden is really dark, turn it into a woodland-style garden filled with shade-tolerant plants.

5 If all else fails, create a focal point that detracts the eye away from the part of the garden you're not so keen on. This could be a really beautiful specimen tree, a water feature or a decorative screen.

DESIGN MASTERCLASS

THE LARGE, EMPTY GARDEN

A vast, uninhabited space can seem intimidating even for the most experienced gardener. You have all this garden to play with, but no structure or plants to inspire you or help you work out how to use it.

Once you've spent some time in it and worked out the key elements, such as where the sunny spots are throughout the day, where you'd like to be screened from neighbours and so on, there are a few simple tricks to try to start breaking down the space bit by bit.

3 of the best...
PLANTS FOR A HERB GARDEN

SALVIA OFFICINALIS
This will give you lots of flowers, becoming big and bushy in no time at all. The ultimate zero maintenance plant that's handy for cooking too.

ALLIUM SCHOENOPRASUM
If planted into a gravel bed this looks especially pretty, giving you small pink flowers and months of tasty chives.

THYMUS SERPYLLUM
A creeping variety that gives masses of soft-pink colour. Cut it back after it flowers in late spring and early summer to maintain its shape.

Style tips

1 Write a list of all the things you want to use the garden for and then start working out which area is suited to what.

2 Next, name areas within your garden. This will help you find purposes for the space, even if it's calling an area of rough grass your 'butterfly meadow' or an overgrown, shaded area at the back the 'wild garden'.

3 Split up your seating areas. Put your dining area in a corner that gets evening sun, and a couple of chairs where you can enjoy your morning coffee. Perhaps you want some seating submerged in a flowerbed too?

4 You don't have to put your table right next to the house – if it's at the back of your garden, it'll encourage you to use more of the space.

5 Adopt different planting styles to break up the space. A herb garden near the kitchen is practical, while ornamental grasses can form the backbone of a low-maintenance border.

TRANSFORM YOUR GARDEN ON A BUDGET | 13

THE LONG GARDEN

So many gardens I see are long and narrow – often attached to townhouses, with uninspiring layouts. Gardens are beautiful when paths lead you to places where you wonder what's coming next. In skinny, rectangular urban gardens you can often, due to lack of design, see everything all at once, which rather ruins the surprise!

But with some clever screening and thought put into how to make the most of all the space, there are lots of ways you can make a boring garden interesting, wild or even romantic.

Style tips

1 Create areas that you can't see immediately from the house, by putting a bench in a bed of planting or screening off a seating area for privacy.

2 Think about creating a meandering path to a secluded spot at the back of the garden. This means you can be more experimental with the layout and create more visual interest.

3 Try not to slice up the garden too much. Think about how the planting and the seating areas can overlap, or play with proportions so your garden looks like it gets bigger towards the back.

4 If you're feeling brave, plant a beautiful tree among long grasses in the central third of your garden with a path through the middle. This will break up the space and make it feel bigger.

5 Offset elements of the garden to make it seem wider. You could stagger flowerbeds through the space so you don't just walk from one end to the other, or use asymmetrical paving through a lawn.

3 of the best... PLANTS FOR SCREENING

PHYLLOSTACHYS NIGRA
Bamboo isn't everyone's cup of tea – some should only be planted in containers to stop them taking over – but this black bamboo is well behaved.

PRUNUS LUSITANICA
The best time to plant a laurel hedge is during its dormant winter months when you can buy it straight out of the ground ('rootball').

ILEX AQUIFOLIUM
The prickly holly is sometimes overlooked in modern gardens, but with berries for birds in winter and evergreen leaves, it's a real classic.

DESIGN MASTERCLASS

THE TINY GARDEN

These days, we all want to get the most out of our outdoor space, be it a balcony, a slither of front garden or a little boxed-in courtyard. However, that doesn't mean you have to create an all-singing garden in one small space.

Instead, refining the elements leads to an elegant and useful area. Less clutter means more room for plants, making it more relaxing. And crucially, you don't have to use small things in a small space; it seems counter-intuitive but sometimes big elements can make it feel larger!

3 of the best... STATEMENT TREES

PRUNUS SERRULA 'TIBETICA'
A beautiful cherry tree that has a rich, colourful and characterful bark. Enjoys full sun and looks stunning in a small garden.

ACER PALMATUM 'SANGO-KAKU'
This acer provides oranges, greens and reds on its bark and leaves. Plant with something black for maximum effect.

BETULA PENDULA
This silver birch is an easy-to-care-for addition to any garden. Plant in the back of a small space to create a focal point.

Style tips

1 Don't be afraid to add drama to a small space, like painting a brick wall in a dark shade. It's easy to overcomplicate a small garden with too much going on.

2 Equally, placing a large specimen tree in a beautiful container will make a focal point of your space – a multi-stem tree is a good option.

3 Small gardens are like little extra rooms in your house, so make sure you can enjoy them even in the winter months when you're sitting inside. Uplights under plants or trees work wonders.

4 Use climbers – there are lots of species that will quickly cover walls and soften your space. Use trellis or wire to train your plants in the desired direction.

5 Think about the colour and texture of hard materials. Large stone pavers can make a space look bigger, especially if they're the same colour as the interior floor in an adjacent room.

TRANSFORM YOUR GARDEN ON A BUDGET | 15

Garden design ON A BUDGET

Ten ideas to stretch your cash outdoors and maximise your plot's potential

Every successful garden transformation starts with planning, so assess your space and work out the key areas that are crying out for some TLC. Is your fence bland and boring and in need of a fresh new look, or is your central focal point a featureless blank wall? Perhaps you've inherited a tired patio that needs an overhaul or overgrown shrubs that need taming?

From simple tips on how to make the most of your garden's features to wise buys and style-savvy additions, follow our dos and don'ts to create the outdoor space you've always wanted – without breaking the bank.

1 DO SPRUCE UP THE GARDEN

'Spring cleaning your outdoor space is a crucial first step when it comes to preparing for the new season, giving you a fresh canvas,' says Marcus Eyles, horticultural director, Dobbies. 'From sprucing up paths and patios to washing down garden furniture, a good clean-up can make all the difference. Neaten beds and borders by removing weeds with a hoe and apply a layer of mulch to give plants a boost for spring.'

Solar Moroccan stake lights, Lights4fun

2 DO GO FOR SOLAR LIGHTING

A few staked spotlights shining up through a tree or a sculpted shrub will create a stunning focal point and add drama too. Alternatively use them along the edge of a border or path to light the way.

GARDEN DESIGN ON A BUDGET

3 DON'T USE TURF FOR A LAWN

If you love the idea of a lush lawn, then you're in luck, as it's relatively cheap and easy to create. Rather than using more expensive rolls of turf, grass seed is the way forward. First, remove any weeds or stones, then rake it level. Lawnmower manufacturer Stihl recommends 'seed coverage of 15g to 20g per square metre'. Water the seeds and keep moist until germinated.

4 DO LAY A DIY PATH

Creating a garden path doesn't have to be an expensive or arduous project. From bark nuggets, slate chippings, gravel or pea shingle, there are a number of easy-lay options that are also practical underfoot and good looking too. First, put down landscape membrane and then the aggregate on top. This will both stop the aggregate from being pushed down into the soil and prevent weeds from growing up, within the path. A thrifty but attractive idea is to lay a woodland-style log path using cross-sections of sawn logs. Place them onto a firmed and levelled pathway and arrange as stepping stones, filling gaps with bark chippings.

For bespoke metal products, try Buy Metal Online

5 DO ADD A WATER FEATURE

Sun or moonlight reflecting off still water is a mesmerising sight and it's easy to bring this dimension to your outside space. Choose a shallow yet wide container – there are some gorgeous metal reflection bowls available – but a vintage enamel basin or even a metal trough will do the job. Place on level ground or raise up on a brick or timber plinth, away from trees or shrubs. Fill with water and enjoy visits from birds and other wildlife.

CREATE RELAXED CURVES OR SHARP-LINED GEOMETRIC BEDS TO REVITALISE YOUR PLANTING

6 DO RESHAPE YOUR BORDERS

Simply altering the shape and size of your flowerbeds can revitalise your garden, costing no more than an hour or two of your time, and a bag of compost. Why not introduce relaxed curves or sharp-lined geometric beds – whatever your design ambitions, a sharp edging tool is a must for this job. Tool specialists Burgon & Ball advise, 'Use borders to create optical illusions: straight beds down either side will make a garden look smaller, whereas a sweeping curve can make it feel bigger. And creating flowerbeds a metre deep allows them to accommodate several different heights of plant for a full, rich look.'

TRANSFORM YOUR GARDEN ON A BUDGET | 17

7 DON'T PAY FOR A NEW PATIO

Rather than forking out for a new patio, simply disguise tired paving or a weathered deck with a colourful all-weather rug. Warm and comfy underfoot, they bring instant pattern into your outside seating space and make a handy focal point to arrange furniture around too. The majority can be left outside during showers and are quick to dry.

Outdoor rugs, from a selection, Dobbies

8 DO SOW A CUT-FLOWER PATCH

Get your greenfinger fix for next to nothing, by sowing a colour-filled patch of annuals. Dig over a sunny site, then scatter a pre-mixed seed selection for a quick growing display. Sarah Raven *Calendula officinalis* 'Indian Prince' and *Echium vulgare* 'Blue Bedder' (sarahraven.com) provides endless cut blooms from May to September and self-seeds freely. Sarah suggests, 'Keep moist until established and apply a liquid feed fortnightly.'

9 DON'T GET RID OF EXISTING SHRUBS

Bring fresh form into your garden by reshaping large, unruly shrubs. Quick and easy to do, it's not only an opportunity to get creative, but can let more daylight filter in, encouraging other plants to grow. 'The best species for shrub topiaries are evergreens with small, dense foliage, such as boxwood, yew shrubs and Thuja conifers,' explains James Ramnought of Phostrogen.

Corten steel planters, Adezz

18 | TRANSFORM YOUR GARDEN ON A BUDGET

GARDEN DESIGN ON A BUDGET

PAINT ALONG THE WOOD GRAIN AND ALLOW 2-4 HOURS OF DRYING TIME BETWEEN EACH COAT

10 DO SPRUCE UP YOUR FENCING

'Painting your fence is an affordable way to spruce up your outdoor area,' says Aaron Markwell, COAT's colour guru. 'Choose a colour that enhances your existing garden. Green tones create an illusion of space whereas a black paint will make your plants pop.'

1 PREPARE THE SURFACE
Give the fence a good clean with sugar soap or mild detergent to remove mould and fix any loose nails. Leave the fence to dry.

2 SAND THE TIMBER
It may seem like hard work, but it will be worth it in the long run as it will help the wood absorb the paint, rather than just sitting on the surface. After sanding, remove the dust with a damp cloth.

3 APPLY PRIMER
While priming isn't always necessary, we'd recommend applying a thin layer with a brush or roller so you can start with a uniform surface.

4 YOU'RE READY TO PAINT
Apply two coats of your chosen top colour, painting along the grain. Using a specialist garden paint or exterior eggshell is best as they can handle harsh weather conditions and won't fade in direct sunlight. Check annually if it needs repainting.

FEATURE JILL MORGAN PHOTOGRAPHS SARAH RAVEN/JONATHAN BUCKLEY; FUTURECONTENTHUB.COM/ GERALD CORBETT, CLAIRE LLOYD DAVIES, ELLY FINDLAY GARDEN, TIM WINTER

TRANSFORM YOUR GARDEN ON A BUDGET | 19

LET IT GROW
'I use the tub for cutting flowers and washing out floristry buckets'

'It's so pretty

COME ON IN!

ABOUT ME I'm Deborah Boston, a florist (@periwinkle.barn). I moved into this Victorian house, just up the coast from Brighton, in 2013 with my husband Jonathan.

THE CHALLENGE The property hadn't been touched since the 1980s and although the garden had a lawned area, it was very unkempt.

THE WISH LIST The plan was to transform the garden into a modern, country space where I could harvest a continuous supply of flowers and plants for my floristry work. I also wanted to install a garden studio at the end where I could host floristry workshops.

'IN FULL BLOOM'

'IT'S SO PRETTY IN FULL BLOOM'

SUNNY OUTLOOK
'Large folding bifolds open to allow a full view of the garden from the new kitchen renovation. Jonathan installed the decked area that leads onto the garden'

Florist Deborah took a neglected back garden and turned it into a modern, country space filled with flowers

A fter years of living in Brighton, we wanted a complete lifestyle change,' explains Deborah, 'so we sold our one-bedroom flat and moved out of the city where we could afford a house with a generous garden. We bought our new home from an elderly gentleman who had lived in the house his whole life. The property hadn't been touched since the 1980s, so we had our work cut out.

'Our plans included building an extension, plus adding a garden studio, so that I could use the space to host floristry workshops outside of the house. Though unkempt, the garden was in a better state than the rest of the house so we decided to keep what existing elements we could.

Planning the scheme

My idea was to transform the space into a modern, country garden. I've got a creative eye and to save money, I was keen to do as much of the work as possible. We kept what we could, including the cherry blossom tree in the middle of the lawn, and worked these existing features into the new design.

Creating a garden full of flowers and plants that I could use in my floristry work was a must, so the plan included widening the borders and planting flowers that would bloom all year long.

Prepping the space

We started by tackling a large sycamore tree and the hedges, calling in the help of a tree surgeon to shape these areas. By far the toughest job was to remove a large mound of earth to make room

TRANSFORM YOUR GARDEN ON A BUDGET | 21

IDEA TO STEAL
'Use foliage and greenery to create natural screening around a seating area'

DOUBLE DUTY
'My vision for the garden studio was to create a space where I could work and also host flower workshops'

NEW USE
'I salvaged the old gate and turned it into my work bench'

BORDER MIX
'Kansa peonies and lupins are really good givers in the garden. Although, the slugs love them too!'

Do it! CUTTING GARDEN

Want to grow your own cut flowers? Try planting these blooms...

✱ **DAHLIAS** These bold, colourful plants are a must for florists.

✱ **PEONIES** Harvest peonies in early summer for floral displays.

✱ **OX-EYE DAISIES** White petals surround a lemon centre. Deadhead regularly to encourage blooms.

✱ **LUPINS** These beauties can be propagated by division.

✱ **ROSES** Plenty of varieties to choose from, and a long vase life.

'IT'S SO PRETTY IN FULL BLOOM'

BOLD CHOICE
'We painted the woodwork black to co-ordinate with the exterior wall colour'

'I COLLECT THE SEEDS AT HARVEST TIME, WHICH I PUT INTO PACKETS TO SAVE FOR THE NEXT YEAR, OR SWAP THEM WITH NEIGHBOURS'

for the garden studio. We found the studio at Skinners Sheds. We built the concrete foundations ourselves, and my dad did the electrics for us. We then painted the exterior of the studio black to match the rest of the house and widened the borders on both sides. Aesthetically, it was important that the exterior of the building project complemented the Victorian house and the newly renovated garden. The extension leads from the kitchen into a living room, with bifold doors that then open out onto a decked area. This new outdoor spot has become an extra living space where we entertain and relax.

Paving the way
A garden path down one side of the plot is laid with grey slate, in keeping with the period style of the house, and continues down the side return. Jonathan also installed decking outside the garden studio to create another sitting area.

At the bottom of the garden there's also an outside prep area, with an outdoor sink and potting bench that were made from the old garden gate and an aged washing tub found at an antiques fair. I try to use reclaimed materials in my garden where I can, like vintage pots, buckets, urns and vases.

Picking the planting
To create an all-year-round display, I filled the beds with grasses inspired by the Sussex Prairie Garden, near Brighton.

Over the years, I then slowly added different types of plants and flowers so the beds accumulated more colour.

Borders filled with flowers and plants of different heights looks natural and lush, and the black-painted fencing creates the perfect backdrop. Every bit of the garden works hard and has provided plenty of homegrown materials for my work. Pottering around out here has been my favourite pastime.

As much as I love the house and garden, having lived here for nearly 10 years, I recently relocated back to my home county of Durham. I've just started growing a flower farm for my new floristry and wedding flowers business. I certainly enjoy a challenge!'

TRANSFORM YOUR GARDEN ON A BUDGET | 23

Zone your OUTDOOR SPACE

Use clever zoning ideas in the garden to create a multifunctional space for the family

GREAT IDEA Paint an outdoor wall black to provide a contrasting backdrop

ZONE YOUR OUTDOOR SPACE

Go for practical built-in seating arranged in a sociable corner setup

Position seating against a backdrop of greenery. Stockholm two-seat sofa, Next

Use... sociable seating

Create an inviting outdoor living area with a comfortable seating arrangement

✶ **CREATE ZONES** Whatever the size of your outdoor space, zoning can be useful to divide the space up into different areas, so there's somewhere to sit and relax, prepare food and entertain or for the kids to play in.

✶ **START WITH THE SEATING** Instead of a randomly placed assortment of furniture, try to group seating in a dedicated area. Choose a spot that lets you take in a lovely view or gives some natural shade, and set up seating in a sociable corner or U-shaped arrangement as you would with an indoor living area.

✶ **MAKE IT MODULAR** For a flexible set-up, go for modular garden furniture that can be arranged to suit the shape and size of your patio area – and easily rearranged if needed. Outdoor pouffes and floor cushions are easily moved around and are handy for extra guests.

✶ **CHANGE THE BACKDROP** A contrasting wall colour or a change of flooring can be a good way of signposting different zones. Paint brickwork or fencing behind seating in a bold shade or go for patterned tiles or an outdoor rug as an anchor point.

Modular outdoor kitchen units are easy to move. Grillskar sink unit and charcoal barbecue, Ikea

Use... *a well-planned layout*

Set up an alfresco cooking area as the hub of your outdoor space

✷ **FIND THE RIGHT SPOT** Whether your outdoor cooking space consists of a trusty barbecue or a brick-built design, choosing the right spot is key. Fairly close to the house makes it easier if electrics or plumbing are required – and avoids a long trek when bringing things in or out of the kitchen.

✷ **WORK WALL SPACE** Positioning an outdoor cooking area along a solid wall makes sense if your patio layout allows and will provide some shelter from the wind when cooking. Wall space is also useful for hanging tools and equipment.

✷ **TAKE SHELTER** Ventilation is a must in any outdoor cooking area, but factoring in some kind of overhead shade will give protection from the elements and keep the kitchen in action all-season long. A timber pergola looks attractive and provides a semi-sheltered spot.

✷ **FIXED OR FREESTANDING** For a permanent outdoor kitchen structure, consider building your own from brick or timber that can be tailored to suit the space. Alternatively, opt for off-the-peg modular units that are lightweight and easily moved around.

ZONE YOUR OUTDOOR SPACE

GREAT IDEA Add wall hooks to hang tea towels, oven gloves and utensils

Choose all-weather work surfaces for greater durability outdoors. Royal real stone work surface, Lundhs

Outdoor kitchen tips and tricks

✹ **TAILOR YOUR SPACE** Start with cooking appliances first, then think about extras that you want to include. Plenty of worktop space for prep is a must and an outdoor sink is a useful addition if you have the room.

✹ **MAKE IT WEATHERPROOF** Surfaces take the brunt of the elements, whether intense heat or excess moisture, so choosing worktops that are weather-resistant, hardwearing and durable is key. Concrete and natural stone, tiles or wipe-clean stainless steel are all good options.

TRANSFORM YOUR GARDEN ON A BUDGET | 27

Play area tips and tricks

✱ **GROW THEIR OWN** Introduce children to gardening at a young age so they can grow their own flowers or veggies. Install a simple raised bed they can tend to themselves, with easy-grow herbs for starters.

✱ **GET MESSY** Encourage creative play with an outdoor mud kitchen for little ones. Buy one off-the-peg or go for a DIY version with a play table and a metal bowl as a sink. Or try an outdoor easel so kids can get messy with paint outdoors instead of indoors.

GREAT IDEA Add pegs to the underside of a sand pit lid to hang toys

Sacrifice a raised bed to create a section of deck with covered sandpit and giant blackboard

28 | TRANSFORM YOUR GARDEN ON A BUDGET

ZONE YOUR OUTDOOR SPACE

Kit out a children's playhouse with favourite things. Tom playhouse, Wayfair

Use... *play space creatively*

Encourage children to spend time outdoors with a dedicated play area

✱ **PICK A PLOT** Whether toddlers or teens, children crave a play space of their own, so if you have the room try sectioning off a separate area. While little ones need to be kept close, a plot at the end of the garden that older kids can escape to is ideal.

✱ **ADD SOME SAND** Children love digging, so set up a sand pit in a corner of the garden where they can play and get messy. Plastic sand pits are cheap to buy or build your own using decking. Avoid positioning in direct sunlight or a damp area and add a lid to keep sand dry.

✱ **BUILD A PLAYHOUSE** A hideaway or den has to be top of most kids' wish lists. Whether you opt for a Wendy house, tree house or outdoor wigwam, let youngsters get involved in the decor, helping to paint the outside in bright colours or cosying up the interior with beanbags, cushions and blankets.

✱ **JUMP TO IT** Garden trampolines are a must-have for little ones, but can be a bit of an eyesore for parents. Setting a trampoline into the ground will make it less visible and easier to access, though a safety net will still be required.

Set up a dining table and chairs under the shade of a pergola

Bring in extra stools to supplement outdoor seating. Alps compact dining modular set, Dobbies

Use... covered areas for dining

Create shaded, breakaway spaces to extend time outdoors when entertaining

✱ **SEEK SHADE** While it's relaxing spending time in the sunshine, some form of shade is a must while eating or entertaining when the sun's at its hottest. Garden parasols are the easiest option and can be stashed away when not in use. Go for a cantilevered parasol that won't obstruct the view across a table.

✱ **GO FOR A SAIL** For a semi-permanent option that's perfect above a dining table, try a simple sail shade. Made from showerproof fabric, it will provide protection from the sun, shelter from wind and create privacy.

✱ **CREATE A FOCAL POINT** While pergolas and canopies are great for adding shade outdoors, they also create a visual focal point that can help to define an outdoor dining area or seating space, making the perfect place to centre entertaining or activities around.

✱ **TRY NATURAL SCREENING** Use outdoor plants and greenery to advantage when creating a secluded seating area or dining zone. Hedges, trees and shrubs can help to screen off seating areas and create more privacy, as well as giving dappled shade overhead.

30 | TRANSFORM YOUR GARDEN ON A BUDGET

ZONE YOUR OUTDOOR SPACE

GREAT IDEA Rig up a sail shade to protect diners from midday sun

Outdoor dining tips and tricks

✱ **CORNER A PLOT** Section off an outdoor dining area with strategically placed furniture. Corner seating will create a natural divide that will help separate the dining area from the kitchen or living zone.

✱ **BRING IN GREENERY** If planting or hard landscaping doesn't give enough privacy, then bring in extra greenery to screen off or separate areas. Use floor-standing planters and tubs, filled with lush, leafy varieties such as palms and large ferns.

USE TO PLANT HERBS

Garden
STORAGE SOLUTIONS

Organise your outdoor space with easy upcycling ideas and repurposed materials

FIX A TRELLIS TO DISPLAY OBJECTS

Leftover trellis panels lurking in the shed? While trellis is a must-have for training greenery or screening an area, it's handy for garden storage too. Cheap, lightweight and easily trimmed to size, add trellis panels above a potting bench for tool storage or attach to the side of a shed and use to display garden bric-a-brac.

RECYCLE AN OLD STEPLADDER

Give a shabby stepladder a new lease of life by transforming it into a plant stand. The tiered steps are perfect for stacking pots, either for storage or display, and it makes a handy space-saver for a small garden. Leave the timber unfinished or paint a shade that ties in with your decor.

While it's tempting to throw away old household items and scrap materials once they've been discarded, why not see if you can salvage unwanted pieces before taking them to the tip? There are plenty of creative ideas that can be put to good use in the garden, from upcycling pallet timber to make outdoor furniture, to repurposing old stepladders to make shelving… all it takes is some imagination.

Start small if you're looking for easy projects to tackle. Spruce up an unused desk or table with a coat of exterior paint to make a handy potting bench. Or stack together a couple of wooden wine crates or old drawers to make storage cubbies for outdoor bits and bobs.

GARDEN STORAGE SOLUTIONS

REPURPOSE A PANEL
Create a handy outdoor storage wall using a couple of slatted panels secured to the side of a shed or exterior wall. Adding S-hooks to horizontal slats creates hanging space that's perfect for hooking up tools and planters. Any slatted item will do, whether a trellis panel or the base of an old cot or bed.

NIFTY HOOK UP

SALVAGE AN OLD STORAGE PALLET
Staple item of many an outdoor project, the trusty storage pallet is a cheap eco-resource for garden DIY with its sturdy timber and solid construction. Upcycle to create basic benches, low-level tables and vertical planters or deconstruct and use the salvaged timber to create bespoke pieces for your garden.

'REPURPOSING OLD OR UNUSED ITEMS PREVENTS THEM GOING TO WASTE AND IS A GREAT WAY OF CREATING UNIQUE AND QUIRKY OUTDOOR PIECES'

LISA FAZZANI, EDITOR OF STYLE AT HOME

GET CREATIVE WITH KITCHENWARE
There are plenty of kitchen items that can be reused – turn old colanders and sieves into hanging baskets, or use pots, pans and even old sinks as planters. Stainless steel funnels (like these) make brilliant twine dispensers – just mount on the wall above a potting bench and thread string through the hole.

FIND NEW USES FOR OLD ITEMS
Before binning pieces that have served their use indoors, see if there's a way of extending their life and upcycling them outdoors. Inexpensive canvas and plastic shoe tidies (like these, right) make great vertical wall planters – simply fill the pockets with soil and potted herbs – or use as a garden organiser and use the pockets for tools, twine and seed packets.

FEATURE LISA FAZZANI PHOTOGRAPHS FUTURECONTENTHUB.COM/ SIMON SCARBORO, JOANNA HENDERSON, ANDREW WOODS, COLIN POOLE

TRANSFORM YOUR GARDEN ON A BUDGET | 33

FACT FILE

✳ **THE DETAILS** Adam Cossey lives here with his wife Irenie and their children, Olivia, Jake, and Clara. Their garden is rectangular and sits behind a semi-detached period house in Islington, north London.

✳ **THE CHALLENGE** To link the exterior seamlessly with the new single-storey extension, which was being built at the back of the house.

✳ **THE PLAN** The family wanted a multi-level design, which was easy to maintain. The children needed space for growing things and ball games, while Adam and his wife could enjoy being out there, too.

GREAT IDEA The parasol means that the levels of sun and shade can be altered with ease

Going GREEN

Re-planning their garden in tandem with building a new extension helped Adam and Irenie Cossey create a flexible outdoor space for all the family

34 | TRANSFORM YOUR GARDEN ON A BUDGET

GOING GREEN

STRONG FOUNDATIONS
The garden boundaries of hedging and shrubs keep the garden looking lush all year round

BORDER FAVOURITE
White cosmos will give plenty of blooms

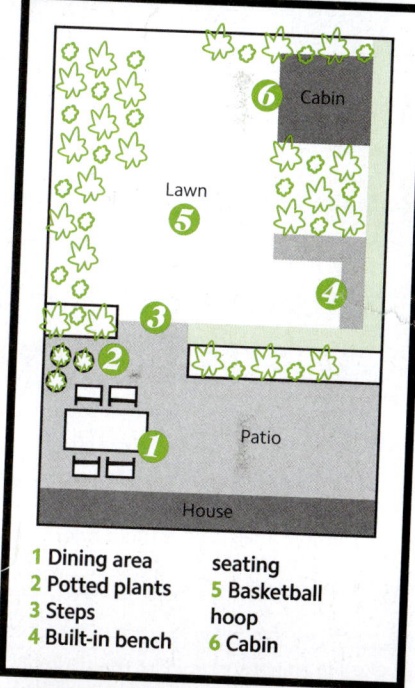

1 Dining area
2 Potted plants
3 Steps
4 Built-in bench
seating
5 Basketball hoop
6 Cabin

"Our plan was for the garden to link smoothly to the interior, so, working with design company Modular (modular.london) we dug down and outwards at the back. This made room for a kitchen extension that could open seamlessly onto a big patio, with steps leading up to the lawn,' says Adam. Bushes and trees lend the garden a leafy, established feel, with ferns and climbers masking the boundary fencing.

A beautiful native hornbeam acts as a focal point at the end of the grass, and planting has been planned to ensure the colour keeps coming from early spring through to autumn. 'I tried to include long-lasting varieties like verbenas and salvias, plus ornamental grasses, to add a bit of height,' says Adam.

By day the garden is a place for everyone to relax, eat and enjoy the outdoors, then after dark, festoon lighting makes for a special atmosphere around the table, while spot lights pick out some of the larger trees. 'Even if it's chilly and the doors are closed, you can have the lights on and still enjoy the garden from inside,' says Adam. 'It makes the house feel larger, too.'

The garden was designed to be a seamless extension of the house, so its

TRANSFORM YOUR GARDEN ON A BUDGET | 35

LITTLE & LARGE
The kids have their own al fresco seating area

STEP UP
The split-level layout helps create different zones

GREAT IDEA
Neat, low-clipped hedges of box add structure to the garden, dividing the patio from the lawn

'CLEAN, SIMPLE LINES REFLECT THE MODERN EXTENSION'

clean, simple lines reflect the modern extension and the interior's contemporary but welcoming style.

A place to play
Tucked in a shady corner at the back of the garden, this pretty pale blue play house, from The Children's Cottage Company, is a fun feature and a big favourite with Adam's youngsters, who enjoy having their own area to play in.

Create zones
Established in a big planter for extra height, fragrant climbers and leafy ferns form a soft, scented backdrop to the dining table, adding an enclosed and inviting feel to the space.

Plant-packed beds, established trees and high hedges make the garden feel lush and secluded, while the split-level layout helps create different zones, adding interest and making the space appear larger.

36 | TRANSFORM YOUR GARDEN ON A BUDGET

GOING GREEN

RELAXING SPOT
The built-in bench creates extra seating

3 of the best...
BORDER PLANTS

✽ ASTRANTIA MAJOR
The variety 'Large White' flowers midsummer and grows to almost 1m tall. Its green-tipped petals add texture and form.

✽ VIOLA
Producing dainty flowers between autumn and spring, these fully hardy plants look charming trailing from planters.

✽ AGAPANTHUS
Also known as an African lily, its globes of trumpet-shaped flowers appear from July to September and enjoy a sunny spot.

Lawn care 101

Basic steps to look after your lawn, from mowing to sowing

For many, a pristine lawn is their pride and joy, but a lot of effort can go into maintaining a grass lawn. We'll share the essential tasks you need to know – and when to do them – to achieve a luscious lawn.

Mowing
Regular mowing encourages grass to grow thick and dense, and keeps the area looking like a lawn, rather than a weed-strewn grassland. Use your lawn mower to trim the grass, and tidy the edges with a strimmer or edging shears.

Mowing does have some downsides. If you mow too often, this can cause nitrogen deficiency in grass plants, and deprives pollinators of the nourishment they can obtain from flowering weeds.

To strike a healthy balance, mow your lawn about twice per month during spring and summer.

Watering
Have you ever seen a satellite image of the British Isles taken during a drought? The land turns a sort of yellowy-brown – and the same can happen to your lawn when the grass doesn't receive enough water.

To keep your grass green and growing, aim to water your lawn on any day without significant rainfall from spring till early autumn. Use your trusty watering can, or set up a sprinkler system to water the lawn like clockwork.

Sowing
Grass seed grows well in mild, moist conditions, so the best times to sow a new lawn (or overseed bare patches) tend to be early spring and early autumn.

Sow the seeds at a density of about 15 seeds per square inch, then water the area generously. Remember to use a cool-season grass variety such as dwarf rye grass, which is well-suited to the UK's climate.

Here are some extra steps you can take to make sure your lawn looks its best:

Aeration
Mowing, watering and sowing are usually all it takes to keep grass alive, but there are some extra things you can do to make your lawn dazzle.

One easy task that every gardener should try is aeration, which means using a tool like a garden fork to make holes in the soil beneath a lawn. The holes help air, water and nutrients to reach grass roots more easily, which can greatly improve the lawn's health.

Aeration does cause some localised damage to grass plants, so it's best to do it in early spring, allowing plenty of time for regrowth.

Dethatching and scarification
Amongst the blades of grass in your lawn is a layer of dead or dying plant matter, known as thatch. There's nothing wrong with a fair amount of thatch, but a layer over half-an-inch thick may prevent healthy growth, or restrict the flow of water and nutrients to the roots.

There are two lawn care processes for dealing with excess thatch: dethatching and scarification. Dethatching is the use of a tool, such as a rake or electric dethatcher with hooked 'teeth' to remove some of the thatch layer. Scarification is a similar process, but uses a more aggressive tool to pull up thatch from greater depths.

Both dethatching and scarification can cause collateral damage to the lawn, so it's best to carry out these processes only occasionally, during a good growing season such as spring or autumn. You'll need to overseed and water afterwards.

Help with lawn problems
A lawn can be a sensitive thing, prone to drought, mould, disease and encroachment by weeds.

If your lawn is discoloured, patchy, or affected by weeds, mosses or fungi, you might benefit from seeking professional advice on how to resolve the problem. Take a photo, and show it to experts such as the staff at your local garden centre, who may be able to identify the proper solution. If all else fails, call in help from a local lawn care specialist.

	MOW	WATER	SOW
JAN			
FEB			
MAR	X		X
APR	X		X
MAY	X	X	
JUN	X	X	
JUL	X	X	
AUG	X	X	
SEP	X	X	X
OCT	X		X
NOV			
DEC			

LAWN CARE 101

3 of the best...
ALTERNATIVE LAWNS

✽ LAWN CHAMOMILE
This voluminous variety of chamomile can be planted to create a dense lawn in low-traffic areas. Instead of mowing, it'll just require occasional pruning.

✽ CREEPING THYME
Creeping thyme takes a few years to get established, but once it is mature it will reward you with a glorious fragrance and annual displays of purple flowers.

✽ MOSS
Mosses encourage biodiversity, and can be walked on like lawn grass. In areas where grasses struggle to grow, consider laying a moss lawn instead.

TRANSFORM YOUR GARDEN ON A BUDGET | 39

Buyer's guide to LAWN TOOLS

Everything you need to keep your lawn at its luscious best

Lawns are among the most plant-dense areas of a garden, made up of countless individual grass plants. All that plantlife takes a lot of tending – especially when you factor in occasional tasks such as dethatching, scarification and aeration, as well as the all-important mowing.

Having a good selection of lawn tools will help you to maintain your lawn more efficiently and effectively. So, let's take a rummage through the shedload of tools that could keep your grass neat and healthy, from lawn mowers to strimmers and rakes.

LAWN MOWERS

Since the invention of the first push lawn mower by Edwin Beard Budding of Stroud, in 1830, keeping a neatly mowed lawn has become accessible to just about anyone who has a garden to call their own.

Considering the fact lawn mowers all have the same purpose, these tools are incredibly varied. That's a great thing for buyers who know what they want from their mower – but not so great for bewildered first-time buyers.

Above all, you need a lawn mower of proven quality. The best way to find out the strengths and weaknesses of an unfamiliar model is to read product reviews from specialist gardening publications and websites, or customer ratings via third-party stockists like Amazon and B&Q. Expert reviews tend to provide lots of detail, while customer reviews offer better insight into long-term performance.

Power source is arguably the most important point of difference between lawn mowers of comparable quality. The three most common sources are:

- **Battery:** removable, rechargeable lithium-ion batteries provide power to a cordless lawn mower.
- **Mains electricity:** household energy powers the mower via a cable and plug connected to a mains power socket.
- **Petrol:** liquid fuel is combusted within an in-built engine to power the lawn mower cordlessly.

Cordless electric mowers tend to provide safe, easy mowing, good energy efficiency and competitive mowing performance. However, their rechargeable batteries will have to be replaced about once or twice per decade, which can come at a steep cost.

Mains-powered electric mowers are the most affordable option, and many gardeners have happily used this type of lawn mower for decades. Of course, the downside is that you'll need to handle a trailing power cable while you mow (and avoid running it over).

Petrol lawn mowers have their special mechanical charms, and they can deliver superb mowing and cordless convenience. With that said, there's extra work involved in maintaining these machines, from annually replacing the spark plug to keeping the fuel tank topped up.

The size and weight of a lawn mower are also key. Look at the mower's specified cutting width for an indication of how quickly it will mow your lawn, and make sure the weight will be manageable for you, before purchasing. Also, check the mower's available cutting height(s), to ensure it can cut grass to your desired length.

STRIMMERS

Strimmers, also known as 'grass trimmers', are made to cut long, unruly grasses and tender weeds. These two-handed tools rapidly spin a length of plastic wire, which powerfully cuts through soft plant matter. The trimming wire gradually wears away during use, and is replenished from a reel housed inside the head of the tool.

BUYER'S GUIDE TO LAWN TOOLS

Cleaning your lawn tools

Grass cuttings, dirt and moisture can cause rust and malfunctions. The lifespan of a lawn tool could range from a few years to decades, depending largely on how well it is stored and maintained. After each use, take a moment to wipe areas such as the cutting deck of a mower, or under the debris shield of a strimmer. Then, store your lawn tools in a dry, safe place.

Choose the right tools to keep your lawn looking its best

Strimmers are great for ensuring neat edges

42 | TRANSFORM YOUR GARDEN ON A BUDGET

BUYER'S GUIDE TO LAWN TOOLS

With this in mind, consider how you will use your strimmer and which features would be useful, before you go ahead and choose a certain model.

Another important factor to consider when purchasing a strimmer is affordability. Most gardeners will use their strimmer only occasionally, so expensive models can come at a very high cost-per-use. Assuming you're not going to take up strimming as a hobby, a highly rated strimmer costing around £60-100 will serve your needs perfectly.

HAND TOOLS FOR LAWN CARE

Many different hand tools still play a key role in lawn maintenance – even though some types like scythes have been superseded by power tools.

Several types of rake can help look after your lawn. One of the most useful is the spring tine rake, which has flexible prongs that can delicately gather up debris such as fallen leaves. (Sometimes, leaf matter is a good nutrient source for the lawn – but not during periods of growth, when grass needs freer access to water and sunlight.)

Some gardeners use another rake, known as a scarifying rake, to scarify their lawn. These rakes have sharp, curved teeth which drag up thatch and moss to create space for fresh growth. A thatch rake is used to pull up thatch – but less aggressively than a scarifying rake.

Instead of buying lots of different rakes for your garden, we'd suggest getting a multi-purpose handle and a selection of compatible rake heads to attach when you need them.

Aeration is another lawn care process that can be carried out using various types of manual tool. For example, you can use a low-cost hollow tine aerator with an array of prongs and a tread plate to stomp holes into the lawn. Charmingly enough, you can also use lawn aerator shoes with spiked soles for the same purpose – or a simple garden fork.

If you're keen to keep the boundary of your lawn tidy, you might want to invest in some edging shears. This cutting tool is used to vertically trim long grass growing out from the lawn edges, with long shanks and handles to keep stooping to a minimum. Edging shears are quite difficult and strenuous to use, but they work much more delicately than an electric strimmer – and usually cost a fraction of the price.

Manual lawn tools do have some downsides. Most require more physical effort than an electric tool built for the same purpose, which is understandably off-putting for some users. Even if you use only one or two hand tools on your lawn, you'll be saving on upfront cost and energy use.

A standard strimmer is the ideal power tool to neaten up most areas of lawn or undergrowth where your mower can't go. Many models are also suitable for 'lawn edging', which means vertically cutting a line around the border of a lawn to prevent messy growth beyond that point.

However, if you have lots of woody weeds around the lawn, you might need a more powerful tool with a stronger cutting wire, known as a brushcutter. These hefty tools are very closely related to strimmers, but feature a higher power output and stronger cutting wire, perfect for trimming thicker, woodier stems.

THE RIGHT STRIMMER

Strimmers come in cordless electric, wired electric and petrol-powered varieties. Cordless electric strimmers tend to offer superior convenience, while wired electric models are ideal for long-duration strimming sessions.

Where strimmers vary most significantly is in their features, which often equip a certain model for particular tasks. Useful extras to look out for when buying a strimmer include:

- Adjustable shaft and grip: allows the strimmer to switch position for horizontal or vertical cutting; or adjusts the shaft length to suit the user's height.
- Guide wheel: helps the user to steer the strimmer accurately while edging the lawn.
- Auto-feeding trimming wire: the trimming wire is automatically replenished during operation.

3 of the best...
LAWN TOOLS

Hot picks to keep your lawn looking its best

Cobra RM4140V Cordless Electric Mower

£354.99, WWW.STORE.COBRAGARDEN.CO.UK

Black + Decker GL7033-GB.700W Corded Electric Strimmer

£77.99, WWW.CURRYS.CO.UK

Wolf Garten UAM Multi-Change Spring-Tined Rake (+ Handle)

£44.99, WWW.WORLDOFWOLF.CO.UK

FEATURE PETE WISE PHOTOGRAPHS ALAMY

TRANSFORM YOUR GARDEN ON A BUDGET | 43

OASIS OF CALM
The white, grey and green colour scheme gives the garden a calm, relaxing feel and helps open out the space. The outdoor table and chairs, from Cyan Teak Garden Furniture, get a lot of use

'We're happy TO POTTER'

Hampered by a lack of green fingers, Susan and Henry Parker hired a professional to turn their small garden into a low-maintenance outdoor room

44 | TRANSFORM YOUR GARDEN ON A BUDGET

'WE'RE HAPPY TO POTTER'

GREAT IDEA
White hydrangeas, foxgloves and variegated hostas shine out in a bed dappled with shade

BEFORE The unloved plot needed a total redesign

FACT FILE

THE DETAILS
Susan Parker lives here with her husband, Henry. Their two adult children have left home. The garden measures 5x7m and sits behind a four-bedroom Victorian house in southwest London.

THE CHALLENGE
The size of the plot meant that seating and planting had to be planned to a T to maximise the available space. So they enlisted the help of garden designer Chris Harrington of Harrington Porter (harringtonporter.com).

THE PLAN
To transform the drab patch of concrete into a space that could be sat in and enjoyed. The planting had to be able to survive with minimal care.

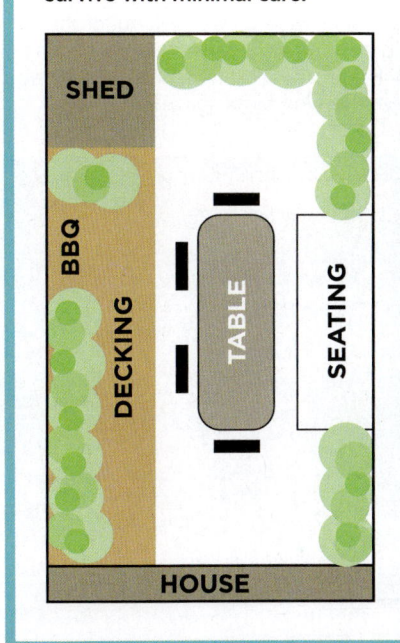

When Susan and Henry Parker moved into their house in 1991, the back garden consisted of cracked concrete, dead plants and an outside loo. They put up a shed, laid a small lawn for their children to play on and built raised beds. 'The lawn was too small and it always seemed to be muddy,' says Susan. In 2000, they built an extension with bifold doors and paved over the lawn, replacing the beds with potted plants. 'Henry and I are no gardeners and we thought pots would be easier to look after than beds, but when we went to Devon for two weeks, we returned to find dead plants!'

Planting scheme
In 2014, they turned to garden designer Chris Harrington of Harrington Porter. 'We asked for a low-maintenance garden with built-in seating, a barbecue, lighting so we could sit outside together in the evening, scented roses and a fig tree, because I love figs,' says Susan. Chris also came up with a planting scheme for the space that includes evergreens and

TRANSFORM YOUR GARDEN ON A BUDGET | 45

perennials that bloom at different times of the year, but require minimal care. 'We're both happy to potter rather than to garden,' says Susan. 'I prune the olive trees, prune and deadhead the roses, cut back the jasmine and mini hedge, and that's about it.'

Living space
The couple have focused on creating a spot for eating and relaxing, with built-in seating and easy-care planting restricted to raised beds. 'It's amazing that such a tiny garden can have so much in it without looking cramped,' says Susan.

Calm colours
White and grey shades were chosen to give the south-facing plot a restful feel. 'We used to have a lot of colourful container plants, but we wanted the garden to be less hard on the eye and more calming'. Outdoor cushions in grey and white stripes co-ordinate with the stone surfaces used throughout the garden as well as with the planting.

The work took a month to complete and Susan and Henry say it was time and money well spent. 'We look out of the kitchen doors and remember that it was such a grotty garden before, but now we have this wonderful space.'

DRAINAGE SOLUTION
Limestone is edged with IPE hardwood decking to break up the white and also to create a porous surface next to the house, which is better for drainage

ALL-YEAR FEASTS
'The gas barbecue was a good investment as we use it all year round,' says Susan

46 | TRANSFORM YOUR GARDEN ON A BUDGET

PERFECT PATIOS

Decking
A smart deck can evoke a holiday vibe at home. Plus, there's a wide range to choose from including rich-toned hardwoods such as iroko, oak and sweet chestnut that last for years if well cared for, treated softwoods and labour-saving composites, which look just like the real thing.

Composite
Low-maintenance, fade proof and resistant to mildew and algae, composite decking creates a smart surface that is smooth and warm underfoot.

PROS
- Choice of textured finishes and colours
- Hidden fixings for uninterrupted finish
- Easy to sweep, scrub and wash clean
- UV stable so won't fade or deteriorate.
- Simple to cut
- Smooth or reeded finish

CONS
- Requires a firm and level base or sub frame
- Boards can appear artificially uniform
- Some cheaper products can have a plasticky feel to them

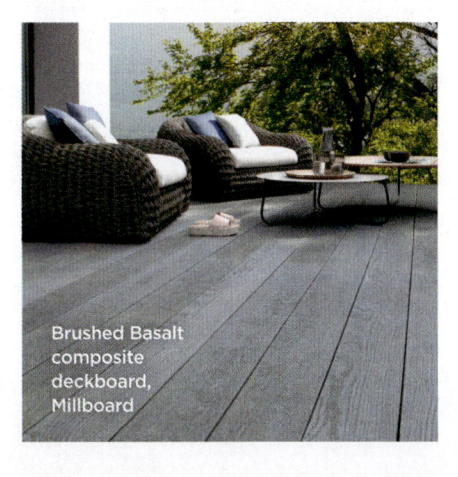

Yellow Balau hardwood decking, Silva Timber

Brushed Basalt composite deckboard, Millboard

Timber decking
Treated softwood boards are readily available and a popular DIY option but they do need careful finishing and regular care to keep them looking their best. Many professionals favour hardwood and cedar timber for a rich, high-end result.

PROS
- Rich tones and natural texture and markings
- Contemporary finish
- Level and firm surface ideal for furniture
- Warm and smooth underfoot
- Wide price range to choose from
- Hardwoods are long-lasting if well maintained
- Easy to sweep

CONS
- Deckboards need a sturdy level base or frame
- Visible joins and fixings
- Requires annual scrub, wash and refinish
- Can require staining and resealing to protect and retain finish

BRICK OR CLAY BLOCKS
Brick or clay blocks always lend a timeless charm to any patio. If laid well, they form a long-lasting and durable surface, that will improve with time and wear. Experiment with different laying patterns from simple stretcher bond to intricate herringbone and basketweave.

PROS
- Frost resistant
- Eco-friendly product
- Can be used to create intricate designs
- Choice of 'bonds' or laying patterns
- Creates a long-lasting, firm, level surface
- Many different shades, colours and finishes
- Easy to sweep and wash clean

CONS
- Ground needs thorough preparation and levelling
- Can be tricky to lay in small or irregularly shaped areas
- Slow to lay – especially when bricks need cutting
- Joins may need topping up with sand

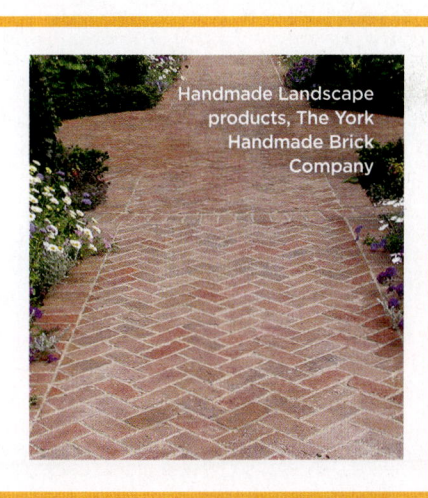

Handmade Landscape products, The York Handmade Brick Company

TRANSFORM YOUR GARDEN ON A BUDGET | 53

Carefully plan your design so you can enjoy it for years to come

Lay your OWN PATIO

Laying a stone patio yourself is cheaper than paying someone to install an expensive alternative and it only takes a couple of days!

LAY YOUR OWN PATIO

Top tip
When choosing your stone patio set try to go for a thickness of at least 2in if the area will be getting a lot of heavy foot traffic. It's better if the surface offers some form of texture to ensure friction

Fill in the surrounding area with gravel or shingle

GREAT IDEA
Consider what colour the stones will be when wet as you might not like it!

Stone is widely available in a variety of patio sets. It can be interestingly textured and comes in an ornate layout. With such a wide range of colours and sizes, paving can be laid in a variety of patterns. There's something to suit every budget, so be sure to explore your options to carefully plan a design that you can enjoy for years to come.

What you will need

MATERIALS
* General purpose mortar (Try cement, Screwfix)
* Set of stone paving slabs in a circular design (Try Abbey York gold circle patio kit, Garden Oasis)
* Optional gravel or shingle to fill in the surrounding area

EQUIPMENT
* Wheelbarrow (for mixing cement)
* Rubber mallet
* Spirit level
* Flat trowel
* Tuck pointer

Preparing your area

* Once you know the dimensions of the patio slabs you've chosen to use, make a detailed plan, so you minimise the need to cut tiles.

* Having planned your patio, it's a good idea to lay the slabs out into position, so you can do one final check of measurements, and ensure you're laying a pattern you're happy with. Take a photo of your preferred layout.

* If your patio is directly next to your house, you'll need to make sure you lay it so that it's 150mm below the damp-proof course.

* To encourage rainwater run-off, your patio should have a fall that runs away from buildings. A 1:60 (16mm per metre) fall is generally recommended.

* If your patio will adjoin your lawn, for ease of mowing, it should sit 10mm below ground level.

* Ask someone to help when you come to lifting the slabs, for both safety and speed of completion.

WORDS: TERESA CONWAY. PHOTOS: GAP

TRANSFORM YOUR GARDEN ON A BUDGET

1 Once you've prepped your area, mix your cement and start from the centre by spreading out an area of cement and laying your first centre slabs.

2 Ensure the slabs are spaced evenly apart and then use a rubber mallet to pat down on the slabs to secure them.

3 You will need an extra long spirit level in order to check that the slabs are lying flat.

4 Once you are happy with the position of the first ring, then you can begin working on the next round.

5 Lay more mortar and place your first slabs with the groove of the previous row roughly in the centre of the slab. If you bought a kit, use the photograph as an indication of how to position your panels. Keep spreading the mortar out with a trowel.

6 Check each position with the spirit level every time you lay a new paving stone. Once you have finished laying all the paving slabs, have a final check whether you're happy with the layout and the gaps, and that they're all flat and even.

56 | TRANSFORM YOUR GARDEN ON A BUDGET

LAY YOUR OWN PATIO

Safety tips

✱ Wear suitable footwear and gloves when handling materials, and when digging.
✱ When using a mortar mix, or Slablayer, wear a dust mask, safety goggles and protective gloves and follow the manufacturer's instructions

7 Using the mortar, tuck pointer and your trowel, it's time to point your slabs. Press the mortar into the gaps in the paving and then smooth off with the blade of the trowel.

8 Leave to dry for around 48 hours and then you can add your furniture and container displays. If you want to, you can fill the surrounding area with gravel.

TRANSFORM YOUR GARDEN ON A BUDGET | 57

Buyer's guide to OUTDOOR COOKING

Broaden your horizons with a barbecue or pizza oven

Cooking outdoors opens up a world of culinary possibilities. In the garden, we can use methods that might not be convenient or safe in the kitchen, such as smoking meat over hot coals on a BBQ, or cooking at super-high temperatures with a pizza oven. There's a vast difference between flame-grilling your food outdoors and searing it in a griddle pan on the hob.

Of course, al fresco cookery can be fun and sociable too. When you have hungry garden guests to feed, there's no better place to work your gastronomical magic than at the centre of the action.

GAS BBQS

Gas BBQs can't be beaten on reliability and efficiency. Fuelled by natural gas products such as butane or propane, these powerful appliances use an array of burners to grill food to crispy perfection.

Most gas BBQs need to be put together from flat-packed parts before use, although some retailers offer professional assembly for an additional fee. Among their core components are grill racks, which are often shaped to sear grill marks into food, gas burners, and a lid that can be closed for convection cooking.

YOUR IDEAL GAS BBQ

Thinking about the scale of your garden get-togethers will help you to narrow down your search for the perfect gas grill, as some models can cater for far larger groups than others. The cooking capacity of a gas BBQ depends on factors such as the dimensions of the grill rack(s), the number of burners and their heat output in British thermal units (BTUs). For big garden parties, you'll need a large, powerful gas BBQ.

Another point to consider is a gas BBQ's features. While no-frills models are relatively budget-friendly, spending a little extra can secure useful add-ons such as an integrated thermometer, storage solutions like racks and side shelves, or metal vaporisers used to recirculate aromatic cooking oils through the barbecue. Battery-powered ignition is a must-have, and a cooling rack fitted into the grill lid will be very useful too.

Quality varies greatly among gas BBQs, so it pays to read some customer reviews and assess the product specs, before deciding on a model. Indicators of good quality include a reputable brand (eg Weber, Char-Broil, Broil King), and premium components such as cast iron grill grates.

Some gas BBQs can be kept outdoors, although we would recommend sheltering yours inside a structure such as a shed during bad weather. At the very least, purchase a well-fitting rain cover to limit the risk of rusting.

BUYER'S GUIDE TO OUTDOOR COOKING

Charcoal is the best choice for that authentic smoky BBQ flavour

TRANSFORM YOUR GARDEN ON A BUDGET | 59

Where to cook outdoors

Shelter plus stability is your recipe for successful outdoor cooking. All barbecues and pizza ovens require a flat, stable surface for safe, proper operation. So, set yours up on a patio, paved yard or purpose-made stand. Some protection from wind will also be useful, as strong gusts can affect cooking performance. A sheltered corner close to a wall would be ideal.

A BBQ or pizza oven is a must if you love to host outdoors

BUYER'S GUIDE TO OUTDOOR COOKING

All gas barbecues run on liquid/gas fuel, but each model will only be compatible with certain types. Check the instruction manual to identify the specific gas product and regulator hose required.

CHARCOAL BBQS
For smoky barbecue cooking, charcoal BBQs will always be king. This classic type of grill uses solid fuel such as lumpwood charcoal to provide heat for grilling and smoking.

Most charcoal BBQs arrive flat-packed, and can typically be assembled using a handful of tools within the space of a few hours. A key difference between models is the available cooking area provided by the BBQ's grill, which usually has a width between about 30-70cm. The greater the cooking area, the more food you'll be able to cook at once – and the more fuel you'll use in the process.

There are two common styles of charcoal BBQ: kettle and barrel. Kettle BBQs are generally smaller, pod-like appliances with good fuel efficiency and a low up-front cost. Barrel BBQs, on the other hand, tend to be great for smoking food, and they often provide plenty of useful, premium features.

When you're cooking over wood or coal, it's likely that one of your aims is to infuse your food with smoky flavour. Try adding some aromatic smoking wood chips – such as hickory, mesquite or apple wood – to the cookfire, as this will create richer flavours and scents.

MEAL-SAVING, USER-FRIENDLY FEATURES
One of the downsides to charcoal BBQs is that it takes practice and patience to get the charcoal properly lit. You can give yourself a helping hand by purchasing a charcoal chimney starter. These inexpensive devices provide optimal conditions for charcoal to catch light, before you tip the burning coals into the BBQ itself.

It'll be easier to maintain the right cooking temperature if your charcoal BBQ has effective temperature regulation features. Depending on the style and model of the barbecue, these could include a chimney, vents, integrated thermometer and height-adjustable charcoal rack.

A wood-burning firepit can also be used for BBQ cooking, provided it can accommodate a suitable grill grate. Firepits don't give you all the same food-focused features as a charcoal BBQ, but they can make outdoor cooking wonderfully sociable, with guests gathered cosily and hungrily around. If you intend to cook with a firepit, choose a model with a height-adjustable grill grate, as this will allow you to tweak the cooking temperature.

PIZZA OVENS
Outdoor pizza oven design has come on leaps and bounds in recent years. A good range of brands now make models capable of rapid, high-temperature cooking, from high-end names such as Ooni and Gozney to budget-friendly brands like VonHaus and Costway. It's a modern yet timeless delight to cook Neapolitan-style pizza – or other slender foodstuffs such as baked camembert and spatchcocked chicken – from the comfort of your garden.

All good pizza ovens deliver extreme heat, with maximum temperatures ranging from around 400 to 600°C. Gas-fired pizza ovens tend to reach very high cooking temperatures quickly and easily, using a fuel such as propane or natural gas. A wood-fired pizza oven delivers superior smoky flavour and a timeless spectacle, but compatible fuels including wood pellets and split hardwood logs are relatively expensive and difficult to light. Meanwhile, electric pizza ovens simply plug into your household electricity.

Some pizza ovens arrive pre-assembled, while others are delivered as a flat-packed kit. A typical model will feature a well-insulated oven void, a narrow opening or door, a chimney flue, and a pizza stone which supports and heats food during cooking.

WHAT MAKES A GOOD PIZZA OVEN?
Using any pizza oven is a real skill – so we'd suggest you choose one with plenty of user-friendly features. Some models now feature a turning pizza stone, which does away with the fiddly task of manually turning a pizza during its short stint in the oven. Other helpful extras include temperature gauges, multiple-zone cooking, and carry handles for improved portability.

Think about aesthetics, too. Pizza ovens often have a pleasing, sculptural form – regardless of whether you've chosen a traditional model with rounded edges, or a sleeker contemporary design. Finishes range widely, from stainless steel and cast iron to brick and clay, so there's plenty of scope to find a model that suits your design scheme and budget.

Of course, a pizza oven's cooking performance is the most important factor of all. For a quick indication, look at third-party customer reviews, and specifications such as an oven's maximum pizza width, heat output rating and the number of layers of insulation around the oven void.

---

3 of the best...
OUTDOOR COOKING PRODUCTS
Our top BBQ and pizza oven picks

Broil-King Royal 320 Gas BBQ
£499.95, THEBBQSHOP.CO.UK

Char-Broil Charcoal M BBQ
£239.99, WWW.ROBERTDYAS.CO.UK

Ooni Karu 12 Pizza Oven
£299, WWW.UK.OONI.COM

FEATURE PETE WISE

TRANSFORM YOUR GARDEN ON A BUDGET

Aldsworth potting table, Garden Trading

FRESH LOOK

Outdoor KITCHEN STORAGE

Organise your cooking kit with these inexpensive garden storage options

There's nothing nicer than eating outdoors with friends and family when the weather is warmer. If you often cook outdoors over the summer months, then having an organised cooking set-up can be a big help and great time saver, with essentials stored within easy reach so there's less to-and-fro indoors and out fetching stuff.

Bespoke outdoor kitchens can be tailored to suit any space, but can work out pricey. For a cheaper option, consider modular concrete units that can be configured to suit the space or try steel flat-pack furniture that can be easily moved around if needed. Or go down the DIY route and build your own brick or timber storage for a bespoke look without the high price tag.

RE-FASHION A POTTING BENCH

Cut costs by repurposing a timber potting bench (or two) into a kitchen workstation. Designed to withstand the elements in pre-treated timber and with steel tops, its sturdy drawers are useful for storing cutlery, linens and barbecue essentials, while bulkier items can be stashed on shelves below.

Grillskar outdoor kitchen island with back panel, Ikea

KEEP IT CONTAINED

Invest in an all-in-one storage unit that can house everything you need if you're really pushed for space. Open shelving is practical for storing cookware, while this clever design includes a useful mesh top panel that features a hanging rail and hooks for utensils, plus slot-on containers for storing oils and condiments.

62 | TRANSFORM YOUR GARDEN ON A BUDGET

OUTDOOR KITCHEN STORAGE

UTILISE FENCE PANELS
In a small outdoor kitchen every inch counts, so put wall space to work with hanging storage for cooking tools and utensils. Slatted fence panels and garden trellis are perfect behind a workbench with S-hooks easily attached so chopping boards, tea towels and other must-haves can be hooked in place within grabbing distance of the workspace.

HANDY HOOKS

Panel and workbench painted in Old English Green garden shades, Cuprinol

BUILD CRATE CUBBIES
Find a new use for old wooden crates by stacking them in multiples to create an open shelf unit. Cubbyholes are super-easy to access and perfect for storing plates, cookware and taller items. Simply arrange crates in stacks to fill the space and screw together to secure. Attach to a shed or fence panel too so they won't topple over.

'CADDIES FOR STORING SMALLER ITEMS LIKE CUTLERY AND CONDIMENTS'
LISA FAZZANI, EDITOR OF STYLE AT HOME

UPCYCLE A PALLET
If outdoor space is tight, make use of wall space to squeeze more in. Try a DIY hack with this simple slimline wall unit made using a couple of upcycled pallets and some lengths of chain. With hidden storage inside, the drop-down work surface is perfect for serving food or drinks and takes up minimal room when closed.

PICK EASY-TO-MOVE PIECES
Set up a run of units alongside your cooking appliance to provide galley-style prep space and storage. Freestanding units are a cheaper option than fixed and are lightweight to lift so can be stored away in a shed or garage over winter. Choose practical coated steel cabinets with stainless steel tops that are easy-clean and won't rust.

Grillskar outdoor kitchen sink unit/cabinet; cabinet, both Ikea

TRANSFORM YOUR GARDEN ON A BUDGET

Well INCLINED

The Rusts made their garden more usable by dividing it into split-level spaces, each with its own look, feel and purpose

64 | TRANSFORM YOUR GARDEN ON A BUDGET

WELL INCLINED

GREAT IDEA
Smart furniture, oversized planters and white and cream flowers create this contemporary cottage garden.

After spending six years renovating their cottage, Judith and Michael Rust turned their attention to the back garden – a rectangular plot that sloped upwards behind the house.

As part of the renovation work, the couple had added a rear kitchen extension with bifold doors and a spacious patio area beyond them. Apart from that, Judith was unsure what to do with the rest of the space. 'It was mainly lawn and there was a very large apple tree taking up lots of room and casting shade over everything,' says Judith. 'It needed a complete rethink. It had to be low-maintenance with some structure and privacy, and I knew I wanted white flowers only, because I love the simplicity.'

She turned to Mike Reeves of Greenman Services, who suggested a split-level design with steps from the patio up to a flat, small area of lawn.

Although the garden is only a few of years old, borders packed with plants make it look lush and established. Perennials and bulbs keep the interest and colour coming from spring to autumn. Ferns, evergreens and annuals like sweetpeas and snapdragons fill the gaps. She's sticking to the all-white theme, but doesn't worry when lilac, blue or pink blooms appear. 'I'm fine with the odd bit of colour, but there was a wrongly labelled yellow rose I couldn't ignore, so I moved that to the front garden!'

FACT FILE

✻ **THE DETAILS** Judith Rust lives here with her husband, Michael. Their outdoor space is a rectangular, split-level cottage garden, in a village in the county of Dorset.

✻ **THE CHALLENGE** Their garden was largely cast in shadow by a large apple tree and had a sloping incline that went up towards the back of the garden.

✻ **THE PLAN** The couple wanted a low-maintenance space with structure and privacy that was an extension of their renovated country cottage.

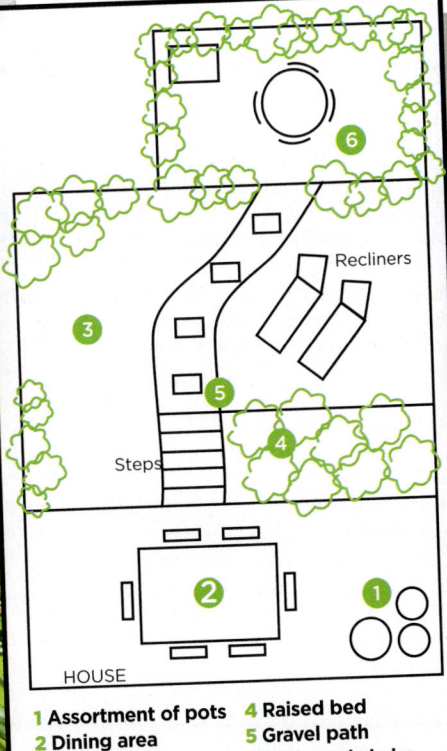

SUPERSIZE PLANTERS
Give a grander, more contemporary look than clusters of small pots

Garden plan:
- Recliners
- Steps
- HOUSE

1 Assortment of pots
2 Dining area
3 Raised lawn
4 Raised bed
5 Gravel path
6 Table and chairs

TRANSFORM YOUR GARDEN ON A BUDGET | 65

THE LAYOUT GIVES THE GARDEN CHARACTER AND DIVIDES IT NATURALLY INTO AREAS FOR EATING, SITTING AND RELAXING

BORDER ORDER
Edging strips keep the gravel contained so it doesn't creep into flowerbeds

Patio dining area
The sunken patio feels enclosed and sheltered, thanks to the retaining walls surrounding the next level of the garden. Judith used the same flagstone flooring inside and outside the house's bifold doors to connect the two spaces. 'We eat outside whenever we can, so the garden's like an extension of our home,' says Judith.

Lawned area
The middle part of the garden is laid to lawn, with steamer chairs for lounging in the sun. Climber-clad trellis fencing screens the garage and the clematis-wound archway gives a glimpse of another small seating area, which catches the evening sun, at the back. This trick makes the plot seem larger than it actually is.

Rendered wall
This was built as part of the garden redesign and provides privacy as well as a modern, Mediterranean feel. In time, it will be mostly covered by clematis and jasmine. It's painted in Farrow & Ball's Bone. 'It's a good match for the patio paving and doesn't compete with the greenery,' says Judith.

Curved pathway
Stepping-stone slabs and gravel create an informal and low-maintenance path. Judith's lush planting spills over to soften its lines. 'Full beds stop weeds taking hold,' she says. 'Our local garden centre sells neglected plants cheaply, so I get them to flourish again and use them to fill gaps.'

Vertical garden
Judith turned an old ladder, bought for a few pounds at a market, into an eye-catching plant stand. 'I like the rustic wood and having plants at different heights – it's a bit of fun,' she says.

WELL INCLINED

3 of the best... MODERN COUNTRY BLOOMS

CLEMATIS
A dainty clematis with pale lilac, bell-shaped flowers makes a hardy climber for softening metal arches or fences.

AGAPANTHUS
Great for attracting bees into your garden, these need little attention and bring height and structure to your flower beds.

SWEETPEAS
Excellent climbers, these are also good for hanging baskets and the flowers are prized for their colour and scent.

SUMMER VIBES
Choose light furniture and accessories for a fresh, summery feel

SECLUDED SEATING
There's a lovely spot for alfresco dining

TRANSFORM YOUR GARDEN ON A BUDGET | 67

1 TRY AN EASY-UP PARASOL

The simplest option if you want to seek shelter outside when the sun is at its hottest, a parasol can be set up practically anywhere to provide instant shade. Choose a size that suits the scale of your garden and anchor it in place with a sturdy base that is heavy enough to ensure the parasol won't tip over in strong winds. Go for a colour that ties in with your garden decor or try a flamboyant design to create a focal point.

Large tassel fringed garden parasol, Staycation Vintage Parasols

Create the perfect SHADY SPOT

Provide a sheltered area so you can enjoy your outdoor space whatever the weather

2 KEEP IT SIMPLE WITH A SAIL SHADE

For a semi-permanent option, consider a sail shade or canopy to give coverage in a corner or section of the garden. Fairly easy to install, position anchor points on poles, fences, the sides of buildings or on a support frame, then stretch the fabric taut to shield the area below from the sun.

GoodHome Grey 3m shade sail, B&Q

Elements 3m cantilever parasol in Teal, Dunelm

3 GO FOR A TILTABLE SHADE

If you're after a parasol for a dining or seating area or you want to create shade around a paddling pool, consider a cantilevered design with a canopy that is designed to hang above furniture. With a super-strong side arm that suspends the shade (rather than a central support), it won't obstruct the view across the table if you're dining or relaxing outdoors. Cantilevered designs are quite hefty so will require a weighted base to keep them stable.

CREATE THE PERFECT SHADY SPOT

4 SET UP UNDER A PERGOLA

For a permanent setup, try a pergola. Generally made of timber or metal, a pergola's open slatted roof won't offer full coverage, but will provide a shady space to escape the full heat of the sun. Growing climbers up and over a pergola will also provide extra natural coverage.

Pergola painted in Ebony Wood Stain + Protect, Protek

'HANG FAIRY LIGHTS ALONG EACH ARM OF A PARASOL TO ILLUMINATE YOUR OUTDOOR SPACE AFTER NIGHTFALL'

5 SEEK SHADE UNDER AN AWNING

Create instant shade at the press of a button with a retractable awning that can be operated by remote control. The perfect solution for a patio area adjacent to the house, the canopy can be extended as and when needed and neatly retracted into a discreet casing when not in use. Added extras include integrated electric heaters, lighting, programmable timers and sensors that will auto-retract the canopy if the weather turns windy.

Breton motorised remote control awning in Wintry Magic, Thomas Sanderson

3 of the best PARASOLS
Keep cool seated beneath a pretty canopy

BOBBLE TRIM
Blue Coral parasol, Oliver Bonas

SCALLOP EDGE
Beige/Green scalloped edge crank and tilt parasol, Daals

PRETTY PRINT
Elder Beach parasol, Wayfair

6 STAY COOL UNDER A GAZEBO

Perfect for parties or as a temporary cover up that can be left outside for the summer months, consider a freestanding gazebo if you're after an inexpensive option. With a lightweight frame and fabric canopy that will give protection against the elements, gazebos are easily assembled (either pop-up or slotted together) and can be stored away out of season.

Gunnon gazebo, Ikea

FEATURE LISA FAZZANI

TRANSFORM YOUR GARDEN ON A BUDGET

Make a stunning OUTDOOR CHANDELIER

Bring a magical glow to evenings outdoors with this fabulous garden lighting idea that is super-simple to put together

Whether dining outside or hosting a summer party, an array of twinkling lights overhead is the perfect way to set the mood and add some extra sparkle after dark.

'A chandelier is a wonderful way to bring atmosphere to outdoor tablescapes throughout the warmer months,' says Lucy Kirk, creative and photography manager at Lights4fun. 'And this DIY chandelier couldn't be simpler to make. Crafted from rustic bamboo hoops and lengths of fishing wire and then illuminated with delicate micro lights and hanging solar bulbs, the end result is enchanting.'

YOU WILL NEED
* 2 bamboo hoops * Fishing wire
* Hook (for hanging) * Set of battery-operated micro lights * Hessian ribbon
* 5-9 solar light bulbs * String

1 ATTACH HANGING WIRES
Begin by gathering two natural bamboo hoops of a similar size. Using fishing wire, attach four equal-length strands around each hoop, securing them in place with knots. Lay one hoop down and gather the loose ends of the wires at the top, tying them together securely. To make it easier to work with the second hoop, we recommend hanging the first hoop from a hook or pole before proceeding.

2 SECURE THE SECOND HOOP
Take the second hoop and attach four shorter strands of wire at each of the four points. Connect the loose ends of these wires to the first hoop, which should now be hanging above. Illuminate the chandelier by wrapping outdoor micro lights around both hoops, ensuring the battery box's cable runs upward for easy hanging, then tuck the box out of sight with a length of hessian ribbon.

3 STAGGER THE CENTRAL BULBS
For the centrepiece, hang five to nine solar bulbs from the lower hoop, using loops of fishing wire at varying heights for a relaxed aesthetic. Enhance the chandelier further by attaching cut flowers along the wires leading to the upper hoop, gathering them at the top and securing with string.

4 POSITION IN PLACE
Once assembled, choose a sturdy location to hang your chandelier – whether it's from a pergola, horizontal pole, or a tree branch over an outdoor table. Make sure it's securely held in place using the top point of the fishing wire, then, as dusk falls, enjoy the gentle glow as the chandelier adds a charming touch to any outdoor setting.

Join the hoops with fishing wire

Snip away any loose ends

Wrap the micro lights around each hoop

Secure the battery box to the hoop

Hang bulbs at differing heights

FEATURE LISA FAZZANI PHOTOGRAPHS LIGHTS4FUN/OLIVER PERROTT

70 | TRANSFORM YOUR GARDEN ON A BUDGET

MAKE A STUNNING OUTDOOR CHANDELIER

Micro battery outdoor fairy lights; hanging solar lights, all Lights4fun

IDEA TO STEAL
Decorate with flowers picked from the garden to add a splash of colour

'CREATE A SPARKLING OUTDOOR CENTREPIECE WITH YOUR CHANDELIER SUSPENDED ABOVE THE DINING AREA'

TRANSFORM YOUR GARDEN ON A BUDGET | 71

Plant-filled HAVEN

Pauline Hamilton has transformed a featureless space into an elegant, contemporary garden, complete with cutting patch, pond and seating

GREAT IDEA
The smooth finish of the sandstone paving provides a clean, unfussy look

72 | TRANSFORM YOUR GARDEN ON A BUDGET

PLANT-FILLED HAVEN

FACT FILE

✷ **THE DETAILS** Pauline Hamilton lives here with her son, Jamie, and her cat Tiger. The plot is a 20x6m garden behind a redeveloped 1930s four-bed terrace in north London.

✷ **THE CHALLENGE** To bring interest to the featureless stretch of parched lawn.

✷ **THE PLAN** To create a clean and contemporary haven for plants which could be used for cut flower displays.

SEASONAL JOYS
'I've mixed evergreen foliage plants, conifers and grasses among the flowers which means the planting looks good all year round,' says Pauline

TRANSFORM YOUR GARDEN ON A BUDGET | 73

3 of the best...
FLOWERS FOR CUTTING

DAHLIA 'SCHIPPER'S BRONZE'
For hits of bold colour in late summer – grows well in pots and borders.

ASTRANTIA
This self-seeding perennial flower is dotted throughout Pauline's garden.

PENSTEMON 'GARNET'
One of Pauline's favourite plants for its long flowering season from May to December.

GREAT IDEA
This small pond makes a good focal point when viewed from the house

SCREEN TIME
The trellis acts as a screen and creates a journey through the garden, as do the paving and steps

74 | TRANSFORM YOUR GARDEN ON A BUDGET

PLANT-FILLED HAVEN

'I LOVE HOW THE GARDEN CAN ALWAYS SURPRISE ME. WHEN I'M BUSY OR RUSHING AROUND, I'LL LOOK UP AND IT STOPS ME IN MY TRACKS'

PICK 'N' MIX
In spring the cutting patch brims with tulips, which are then replaced by dahlias for late summer and autumn

When Pauline Hamilton was looking for a new home six years ago, some things were non-negotiable. 'The house had to be a renovation project with the garden a blank canvas, and it had to face south,' she says. 'I really wanted a place which had the sun.' She found her dream in Bounds Green, north London, and immediately set about the refurbishments.

'The garden was nothing more than a stretch of lawn with an old apple tree in the middle,' says Pauline, who had her heart set on a contemporary style which would also allow her to indulge her love of plants.

Having studied garden design a few years earlier, she drew up a detailed plan, which the contractors built within a couple of weeks and which Pauline subsequently planted.

Chic design

Paving leads the way through the space, with deep beds adding intrigue as taller plants veil parts of the garden beyond.

The smooth sandstone and rendered walls create a chic, sleek look, enhanced by the restrained black and white colour palette. 'The builders were horrified by the black fences,' laughs Pauline, 'but as soon as they were finished, they loved it – it's such a good contrast to the plants.' These include glossy evergreens, airy grasses and lots of flowers, especially dahlias, to which she has devoted an entire bed in the cutting patch at the rear of the garden. 'I love having flowers in the house,' she says, 'and this allows me to do that without having to worry about ruining my view.' The dahlias are at their best in late summer.

Pauline divided the garden into three sections, with a deep planting bed close to the house to 'bring the garden in' and a trellis towards the rear. This screens the cutting patch, meaning the whole space cannot be seen at once.

Raised beds

These beds have been a revelation for Pauline. 'After so many years of digging in London clay, these are more like a sandpit,' she laughs. The plants enjoy them too, with many of her tulips returning year after year.

Contrasting effects

'The hard landscaping is simple and rectilinear and makes a good contrast with the informal planting,' says Pauline. 'Because you can't see the whole space at once, it also leads you on a journey.

'Don't be afraid to dig plants up and move them around – or even to replace them – if you don't get it right first time. It's better to act quickly than to wait and see.' (@paulinesplantsandposies).

FEATURE AND PHOTOGRAPHS FUTURECONTENTHUB.COM

TRANSFORM YOUR GARDEN ON A BUDGET | 75

The bluffer's guide to SOIL

SHADY AND DRY

This is a difficult garden area in which to establish plants and only a limited few survive with no watering.

Vinca major is a trailing spreader for tough spots

Helleborus orientalis – a flowering perennial

Epimedium latisepalum has dainty flowers

Heuchera 'Marmalade'

PERFECT PLANTS

GROWING TIPS

● Before planting, dig a deep hole part-filled with compost, and thoroughly soak the plant's rootball. Water new plants weekly until they are established.

● Under deciduous trees, plant spring-flowering bulbs such as cyclamen, anemones, snowdrops and narcissi.

● Create a ground cover of foliage to retain moisture.

● In spring and during hot spells, thoroughly soak the ground once every ten days – this encourages deep root penetration, whereas watering little and often develops weak, shallow-rooted plants.

● If planting in terracotta pots, line them with plastic to retain moisture in hot spells, adding moisture-retentive gel granules to the compost.

● Dig in organic matter to increase the moisture retention of the soil, mulching heavily with a thick layer of bark chippings in spring.

HEAVY WET CLAY

Easily recognised because it is sticky and lumpy when wet, draining poorly, but bakes rock hard and cracks in full sun.

Arum lilies are happy in boggy soil

Moisture lover: Iris pseudocorus or yellow flag iris

Michaelmas daisies

Helenium is reliable in heavy clay

PERFECT PLANTS

GROWING TIPS

● Improve the drainage by digging in as much horticultural grit, sharp sand or even fine gravel dredged from freshwater sources as you can muster – around one bucketful per square metre.

● After digging deeply, build raised beds to a minimum height of 25cm for plants that cannot survive with wet roots, with brick walls or timber beams to retain the soil, and fill with a topsoil rich in decayed organic matter (loam).

● Mulch heavily with compost in spring to retain moisture and reduce surface cracking.

● This soil is nutrient-rich and is ideal for late-flowering perennials such as helenium, aster and bergamot.

● If an area is permanently moist, possibly because of a high water table or nearby spring, consider a 'bog garden' with large-leaved plants such as gunnera.

Acid or alkaline?

Soil pH can influence what will flourish. How to tell? Ask a neighbour or buy a pH testing kit to check

ACID Some of the most attractive flowering plants, such as azaleas and camellias, love acid soil, and will suffer if soil is too alkaline as some nutrients become locked up. The first sign of iron and magnesium deficiency in such shrubs is yellowing leaves. If you are unable to grow these lime-hating plants in the ground, plant them in containers or beds filled with ericaceous compost.

Himalayan blue poppy

Camellia x williamsii

Azaelea

76 | TRANSFORM YOUR GARDEN ON A BUDGET

THE BLUFFER'S GUIDE TO SOIL

SANDY AND FREE-DRAINING

These soils lack sufficient moisture and nutrients to keep all but the hardiest plants going during hot summers.

PERFECT PLANTS
- Echinops ritro 'Veitch's Blue'
- Echinacea purpurea 'Doubledecker'
- Kniphofia 'Pineapple Popsicle'
- Verbena bonariensis

GROWING TIPS

- To give plants the best start, pour compost into each planting hole to the depth of the head of a spade.
- Weeds must be kept tightly under control. For minimal maintenance, cover the earth with a weedproof, semi-permeable membrane, securing it with stakes, then cut slits to plant through. Once planted, cover the membrane in a 3cm depth of gravel.
- Mediterranean plants such as rosemary and lavender cope well, surviving on impoverished soils. Their small, waxy leaves reduce moisture loss.
- As these soils are dry and warm in early spring, they can be ideal for sowing early vegetable crops.
- The finer the particles in sandy soil, the better it will retain water. If you have such a soil, you can expect very healthy plants.

HOT AND SUNNY

These will be areas like a south-facing bed or border that get the full heat of the sun all year round.

PERFECT PLANTS
- Hibiscus are hardy
- Aeonium arboreum 'Zwartkop'
- Cannas give an exotic feel
- Abutilon 'Orange Hot Lava'

GROWING TIPS

- Grow easy ground-cover plants such as nasturtiums or osteospermums to keep the surface of your soil shaded and cool.
- Sunny plots are ideal for many herbaceous favourites – roses, bergamot and tobacco plants, for example.
- They are also perfect for hot-coloured tender exotics such as cannas and ginger lilies, but grow them in large plastic pots that, come spring, are submerged in beds, but can be lifted in autumn and overwintered in a greenhouse to avoid frosts.
- Lay a hose with small holes punched along its length through the bed, to drench the soil in the evening when needed during particularly hot spells.
- Train tender climbers such as abutilon or flame creeper up obelisks, to add height and structure in winter.

ALKALINE

Soil over chalk or limestone is usually alkaline and is often rich in calcium. It has good drainage but can be thin and requires copious amounts of organic matter such as home-made compost or well-rotted manure added to retain moisture. When planting on chalk, break up the ground to a depth of 75cm to allow plants' roots to spread. A good tip: smaller plants establish quicker than mature ones.

Verbascum — Honeysuckle — Euonymus

TRANSFORM YOUR GARDEN ON A BUDGET | 77

1

50 *great value plants for* BUDGET GARDENING

A beautiful and productive garden needn't cost the earth, simply choose the right plants

50 GREAT VALUE PLANTS FOR BUDGET GARDENING

BULBS, TUBERS & CORMS
Not only great value, there's a bulb for every season. Check catalogues and look online for good deals

7 DAHLIA
Dahlias can be relied upon to flower for months, and are economical if bought as tubers. Start them off in pots of compost in February and plant out in May. **H90cm**

8 AUTUMN CROCUS
Bring a spring-like freshness to the garden in Oct-Nov with this crocus that is the source of saffron, gathered from its three long red stigmas. In August, plant corms 10cm deep in gritty, well-drained soil in full sun. **H15cm**

9 IRIS RETICULATA
Bringing a welcome sight in early spring, Iris 'Katharine Hodgkin' appears delicate, but is in fact robust and vigorous. A great value bulb guaranteed to give years of pleasure. **H15cm**

Top tip Grow biennials for a bee-friendly garden

BIENNIALS
For a succession of flowers in spring and summer next year, start off biennials in trays from May-July and plant out in the autumn

1 HOLLYHOCK
This perennial is best started from seed one year for flowers the next. Sow seeds in pots and plant the following spring in a sheltered spot. **H90-120cm**

2 SWEET WILLIAM
Perfect for pots and borders, the densely packed sweetly scented flower heads come in a combination of pink, red and white. Grow in full sun. **H60cm**

3 CANTERBURY BELLS
Lofty stems with white, pink or blue bell-shaped blooms add elegance. Start seeds off in seed trays and transplant to their flowering positions in autumn. **H90-120cm**

4 ERYNGIUM GIGANTEUM
Happy if given plenty of sunshine and tolerant of dry soils, the branching heads of silver flowers appear above large heart-shaped leaves. Start seeds in pots. **H1m**

5 FOXGLOVES
The classic biennial *Digitalis* produces spires of thimble-shaped bell flowers with speckled throats, that are great for bees. **H1.5m**

6 FORGET-ME-NOT
A delight in spring when sprays of tiny blue flowers froth around spring bulbs. For a change, try pink or white flowered varieties – simply sprinkle seeds where they are to flower, and they readily self-seed. **H20cm**

TRANSFORM YOUR GARDEN ON A BUDGET | 79

ANNUALS

Annuals are an affordable way to fill containers and plug gaps in your borders. Make successional sowings for a longer display, or choose online mail order plug plants, but be sure to compare prices and delivery charges

10 CORNFLOWER
A cottage garden favourite that comes in pink, white or blue, look for the more unusual 'Classic Magic' (shown). Collect seeds to store in envelopes for the following year. **H1.2m**

11 COLEUS
A perennial grown as an annual. Take one sturdy plant and cut stems as cuttings to fill summer containers. Site in semi-shade and nip out the flowers to keep bushy. **H40cm**

12 LAVATERA
For impatient gardeners who want non-stop colour, this quick-growing annual becomes a mass of pink trumpet blooms. Ideally planted in full sun and perfect for dry soils. **H75cm**

13 CALENDULA OFFICINALIS
One of the best budget hardy annuals, sow once and it'll pop up every year. Pot marigold is a useful companion plant to repel tomato and bean pests, the petals are edible. **H45cm**

14 ESCHSCHOLZIA
Californian poppies are one of the easiest plants to grow, simply sprinkle into gravel gardens or borders and plants will self-seed. Single blooms appear above ferny blue-green foliage. **H30cm**

15 PHACELIA TANACETIFOLIA
This annual has an architectural beauty with its unfurling cymes on strong stems that make good cut flowers. The scented flowers are magnets to bees. **H45cm**

16 NICOTIANA SYLVESTRIS
Statuesque tubular white flowers provide a heavenly evening scent. Easy from seed, start in pots and transplant. Plants will self-seed in milder regions. **H1.5m**

Top tip Keep cutting and more flowers will come

CLIMBERS

Climbers are great value plants for their incredible vigour and sheer flowering ability – they bloom continuously throughout summer and into autumn

17 CLEMATIS
Perfect for tubs or borders, there are hundreds of clematis varieties available in many colours. Check supermarkets for large-flowered varieties, such as 'Hagley Hybrid'

18 IPOMOEA LOBATA
At its peak from late summer to autumn, this tender climber likes a sheltered, sunny spot. Start seeds in pots and plant out in May. **H2m**

19 ROSE
No garden is complete without a rose, look for repeat-flowering varieties such as 'Climbing Iceberg' as bare-root to plant from November-March. **H3.5m**

80 | TRANSFORM YOUR GARDEN ON A BUDGET

50 GREAT VALUE PLANTS FOR BUDGET GARDENING

Top tip
Split with a sharp knife multiple times to increase your plants

Top tip
Check budget supermarkets for bargain buys

Top tip
Lift and split roots in spring or autumn to increase your plants

GRASSES
Grasses and sedges are grown for their foliage and smaller size, and like to be divided every few years, which is perfect when gardening on a budget

22 FESTUCA GLAUCA
This vibrant evergreen grass can be grown from seed, the leaf colour intensifies with sun and drought. **H15cm**

23 STIPA TENUISSIMA
Tactile, flowering stems of the pony tail grass sway in the breeze. Plant in a sunny spot in well-drained soil, they'll seed around. **H60cm**

24 UNCINIA 'EVERFLAME'
Guaranteed to brighten a dull corner, this tough evergreen sedge makes a spreading mound and perfect pot plant. Prefers moist soil. **H30cm**

25 ANEMANTHELE LESSONIANA
The pheasant grass is a star for dry shade and pots, its leaves changing through reds, oranges and greens topped by tiny cascading flowers. Evergreen, readily self-seeds. **H1m**

HERBS
Herbs fit nicely into a mixed sunny border. These easy perennial herbs are widely available as young plants and are cheap to raise from seed

26 FENNEL
What better sight in summer than umbels of yellow flower heads covered in insects. Leaves have an aniseed flavour, collect the aromatic seeds while still green. Readily self seeds. **H1.5m**

27 THYME
There are so many thymes to choose from, some form attractive little mounds, others are ideal gap fillers between paving, such as the creeping T. serpyllum (shown). **H8cm**

28 OREGANO
A small pot from the garden centre will spread and increase to make a substantial clump. Cut back after flowering and propagate by cuttings or division. **H50cm**

20 LONICERA 'SEROTINA'
Not all honeysuckles are scented, but this one produces a lovely strong fragrance. Good for wildlife, flowers for a long period, and plants are usually available for under £8. **H7m**

21 PASSIFLORA CAERULEA
Passion flowers are much tougher than you'd think. These tendril climbers require initial support against a warm fence or wall. Easy to propagate from cuttings. **H9m**

TRANSFORM YOUR GARDEN ON A BUDGET | 81

Top tip When taking cuttings, always prepare a few more than you actually

PERENNIALS
Perennials flower for several weeks. To get the best value, choose plants that are easy to divide or grow from seed

29 ERIGERON KARVINSKIANUS
For flowers from spring to winter, look no further than Mexican fleabane. Masses of small white and pink daisy blooms are perfect for pots. **H30cm**

30 LYCHNIS CORONARIA
From grey, felted rosettes rise magenta flowerheads that easily self seed, look for the white 'Alba'. Prefers well-drained soil. **H75cm**

31 ERYSIMUM BOWLES'S MAUVE
This short-lived wallflower takes the prize for an extended display if planted in full sun. **H75cm**

32 ALCHEMILLA MOLLIS
Lady's mantle is a useful self-seeder for filling gaps in paving and borders, producing frothy, lime green flowers. **H50cm**

33 SEDUM HYLOTELEPHIUM
One of the easiest plants to grow and propagate in early summer. Intense ruby-red flowers are a highlight of autumn. **H50cm**

34 RUDBECKIA
A bold beauty that requires little attention. **H60cm**

35 SALVIA MICROPHYLLA
Renowned for being one of the longest flowering and easiest to grow plants. **H90cm**

TREES & SHRUBS
It's a false economy to buy larger specimens that may struggle to establish compared to smaller versions. Choose a mix of deciduous and evergreen plants that will perform over a long period

36 HOLLY
Perfect as a hedging plant. Buying a quantity from a specialist supplier makes economic sense, plants are smaller than garden centre plants but are more affordable. Try hedging.co.uk. Heights vary.

37 EUPHORBIA CHARACIAS
Shrubby euphorbias can be found at very affordable prices online, look out for those with attractive variegation. In spring each stem is topped by heads of greenish bracts that last for months. Prefers well-drained soil. **H1.2m**

38 HIMALAYAN BIRCH
This stunning tree offers a quick to mature screen with dazzling white bark. Small saplings will establish quickly in any soil. See online mail order for multi-stemmed trees for around £20. **H8m**

39 BUDDLEJA DAVIDII
The sun-loving bush is a magnet to butterflies and produces an abundance of flowers for months on end if diligently deadheaded. Thrives in dry soil and a sunny spot. **H2.5m**

40 EUONYMOUS ALATUS
The winged spindle bush turns glorious shades of crimson and red in autumn. For small gardens try 'Compactus', ideal as a low hedge or for growing in containers. **H1m**

82 | TRANSFORM YOUR GARDEN ON A BUDGET

50 GREAT VALUE PLANTS FOR BUDGET GARDENING

Top tip
Split the cost of buying packets and seed potatoes with friends and family

GROW YOUR OWN
It's more economical to grow from seed, plus open-pollinated varieties (non F1 hybrid) are cheaper to buy and can be saved year after year

41 POTATOES
Grow 'earlies' that crop when potatoes are at their most expensive. Plant seed potatoes in old compost bags or in the ground to save compost, in succession from March to April.

42 SALAD LEAVES
Harvest loads of cheap organic salad leaves with cut-and-come-again types and baby leaves. Make successional sowings from March-September, in pots or trays.

43 TOMATOES
Grow fewer plants well and concentrate on quality. Try 'Gardener's Delight' or cherry 'Sungold' for flavour. Start seeds off indoors from end of Feb.

44 SWEET CORN
Cheaper to grow than to buy and it tastes much better. Open-pollinated varieties adapt well to different soils and climates, try organic seeds of the supersweet 'Damaun'.

45 FRUIT TREES
Small fruit trees and bushes are economical to buy as bare roots and usually establish well. Red and blackcurrants can be multiplied by taking cuttings.

46 COURGETTES
Prolific croppers, one plant can produce 15-20 courgettes in the ground. Regular picking will encourage more to come.

HOUSEPLANTS
Many great foliage house plants are good investments for being long-lived and self-propagating. Check out value supermarkets and DIY stores for bargain plants

47 RUBBER PLANT
Seriously uncool for a time, but *Ficus elastica* has come back into fashion. The solid colouring works alongside other houseplants. Plant in a well-lit spot, water only when dry. **H3m**

48 DRAGON TREE
Dracaena marginata will give a sculptural look and can be picked up cheaply. Tolerant of low light, if it begins to look lanky, start new plants by cutting stems into sections. **H90cm**

49 TRADESCANTIA
A graceful trailing houseplant for a shelf or indoor basket, pinch back the branches to keep the plant bushy and use as cuttings that will root quickly in water. Keep moist and well lit.

50 SUCCULENTS
For little outlay there are many types to choose from – aloe, haworthia and crassula plants look attractive grouped together in shallow ceramic bowls of gritty compost. **Heights vary.**

TRANSFORM YOUR GARDEN ON A BUDGET

A *family* AFFAIR

With spaces for eating, socialising, alone time and hobbies, Tracey James and Paul Roye have created a garden specially designed to suit every member of their family

FACT FILE

✱ **THE DETAILS** Tracey James lives here with her partner Paul Roye and their three grown-up children.

✱ **THE CHALLENGE** A plot belonging to a four-bedroom Victorian house in north London. 'It was definitely money well spent, as well as an enjoyable project. Everyone loves the garden now and we're out here all day in summer.'

✱ **THE PLAN** The garden has three sections – the top patio, which is bathed in morning sunshine, the central seating area and the bottom deck with a water feature, and Tracey's 'she shed', which she uses for her crafting activities.

BEFORE

1 Table and chairs
2 Potted tree ferns
3 Built in bench
4 Path
5 Water feature
6 Hanging chair

84 | TRANSFORM YOUR GARDEN ON A BUDGET

A FAMILY AFFAIR

GREAT IDEA
Use alliums to add height to borders with their structural stems and pom-pom heads – and they attract bees, too

'THE SEATING CONTAINS THE MAJORITY OF THE PLANTING, WHICH WAS CHOSEN FOR ITS HEIGHT, MOVEMENT AND STRUCTURAL SHAPES'

Tracey James' previous garden consisted of a patio, lawn, path and a tumbledown shed. 'I wanted more interest, and a crisp, architectural feel,' says Tracey, 'As our grown-up children live at home, it was about creating a relaxing, low-maintenance, adult space for everyone. Another must-have was a shed for me to keep my sewing machine and fabrics.'

Help from the pros
Acting on a recommendation, Tracey and her partner Paul contacted Sakura Gardens (www.sakuragardens.co.uk). 'Paul and I already had ideas about the planting and other things we wanted, like the water feature,' says Tracey. 'Sakura's designers pretty much hit the brief first time, with just a few small tweaks needed here and there.'

Perfect aspects
The movement of the sun from the patio to the far end of the garden helped dictate the new layout. The seating was placed centrally, where it would enjoy almost all-day sunshine. Its linear design was carefully measured to give the illusion of regular, straight lines, as the garden is not quite a perfect rectangle.

Planting scheme
The seating also contains the majority of the planting, which was chosen for its height, movement and structural shapes. 'We've planted white flowers, like alliums and lilies, but it's mostly about textures and greens. I love the palms and grasses

TRANSFORM YOUR GARDEN ON A BUDGET | 85

TALL...
Tall alliums are a recurring feature

...BRIGHT...
Call lilies continue the white theme

...& HANDSOME
Tree ferns in pots make a statement

we chose, especially the variegated and blue-toned ones,' says Tracey.

The work was an investment, but it's made the outdoor space much more usable and enjoyable, as well as improving the flow and the feeling of space in the ground floor of our house.'

Dining space
A round dining table maximises space on the raised patio, which has a full view of the whole garden. Steps lead down to the stepping-stone path. 'We discussed using artificial grass,' says Tracey, 'but I'm glad we went for the real thing – it's authentic and natural.'

Mini waterfall
The water feature is built into the deck at the end of the garden. A twice-yearly treatment with protective teak oil keeps the yellow balau hardwood looking smart and glossy.

Seating area
Benches have been built into the concrete planting troughs to make them look as if they're floating above the ground. White gravel underneath them emphasises the effect, also avoiding unsightly strips of discoloured lawn where the sunlight might not reach.

86 | TRANSFORM YOUR GARDEN ON A BUDGET

A FAMILY AFFAIR

3 of the best... GRASSES FOR FILLING GAPS

SWITCHGRASS
A stiff, upright grass that can grow to about 1.5m in height, with blue-green leaves that gradually turn yellow in autumn. Plant in clumps for maximum impact.

JAPANESE FOREST GRASS
A compact, easy-to-grow grass with yellow leaves, striped with bright green. Cut back in winter to encourage new spring growth.

EULALIA GRASS
This bushy grass has fine green leaves through spring and summer, and develops feathery, creamy-brown flower heads for autumn interest and texture.

'NTING AND DESIGN, AND A WHATSAPP GROUP IDEAS AND IMAGES'

TRANSFORM YOUR GARDEN ON A BUDGET | 87

Buyer's guide to GARDEN STRUCTURES

How to build livability into your outdoor space

Most garden designers would agree that the best gardens intertwine the beauty of nature with life-enhancing human considerations. To that end, structures like summer houses and arbours can plant comfort and shelter right in the heart of your garden, extending the sense of home into the outdoors. Other types, such as pergolas and arches, add rhythm to a garden design, while expanding growing space skywards.

Some handy households build their own garden structures from scratch, but the simpler option is to choose a flat-packed or pre-assembled model, delivered by a retailer. You're buying for the long-term, so it pays to make a well-considered choice.

SHEDS

The deeper your love of gardening, the more likely you are to benefit from a garden shed. Used to store tools and materials since antiquity, these simple structures help gardeners to keep things safe and orderly.

Most sheds are made from softwoods like larch or spruce, with a pitched roof covered by a waterproof material such as shed felt. Flat-roofed sheds are lower-cost, but may become leaky as the structure ages.

WHICH SHED IS RIGHT FOR YOU?

Sheds vary in their assembly requirements. While some skilful households create their own garden shed from purpose-bought materials or salvaged scrap, many prefer the lower-stress option of buying a professionally designed structure. You can save money by buying your shed flat-packed, then assembling its components using a modest range of tools. Alternatively, some retailers will be happy to assemble or install your ready-made shed for an additional fee.

What will you keep in your shed? There are countless answers to this question: rakes, hoes, barbecues, lawnmowers, sacks of compost, containers, that broken toaster you've been meaning to recycle, and just about anything else that needs to stay dry. Choose a shed with adequate dimensions to store your outdoor inventory, while allowing some walking room for access.

Another factor is which structural features your shed should have. Depending on your needs, you might look for a shed with shelving, a work-bench, integrated vertical bicycle storage, or a ramp for easy wheelbarrow access. Some sheds have windows, which tend to make the space easier to use – but also easier for burglars to break into.

Speaking of whom, it's worth considering your shed's level of security. If you plan on storing valuable tools in your shed, or if your outdoor space is easy to access, then it'd be prudent to choose a shed that has a robust lock and sturdy hinges on the door. Installing a security camera or light will help, too.

A shed can be more than a mere storage facility. If there's enough room inside, you can make homely additions such as seating, a table and other furnishings. Could there be a better quiet spot to pot up plants, drink a cup of tea or do some reading?

SUMMERHOUSES

If a shed can be homely, a summerhouse can be palatial. These human-first garden structures are purpose-made for outdoor living, providing a dedicated space for relaxation and enjoyment.

Most summerhouses are sold as a flat-packed kit – with or without an assembly service included. Styles vary widely, from simple, shed-like structures with generous windows and doors, to chalet-style buildings featuring

Summerhouses offer a space to relax and enjoy your garden

Trellised arbours are ideal for growing climbers, such as wisteria

88 | TRANSFORM YOUR GARDEN ON A BUDGET

BUYER'S GUIDE TO GARDEN STRUCTURES

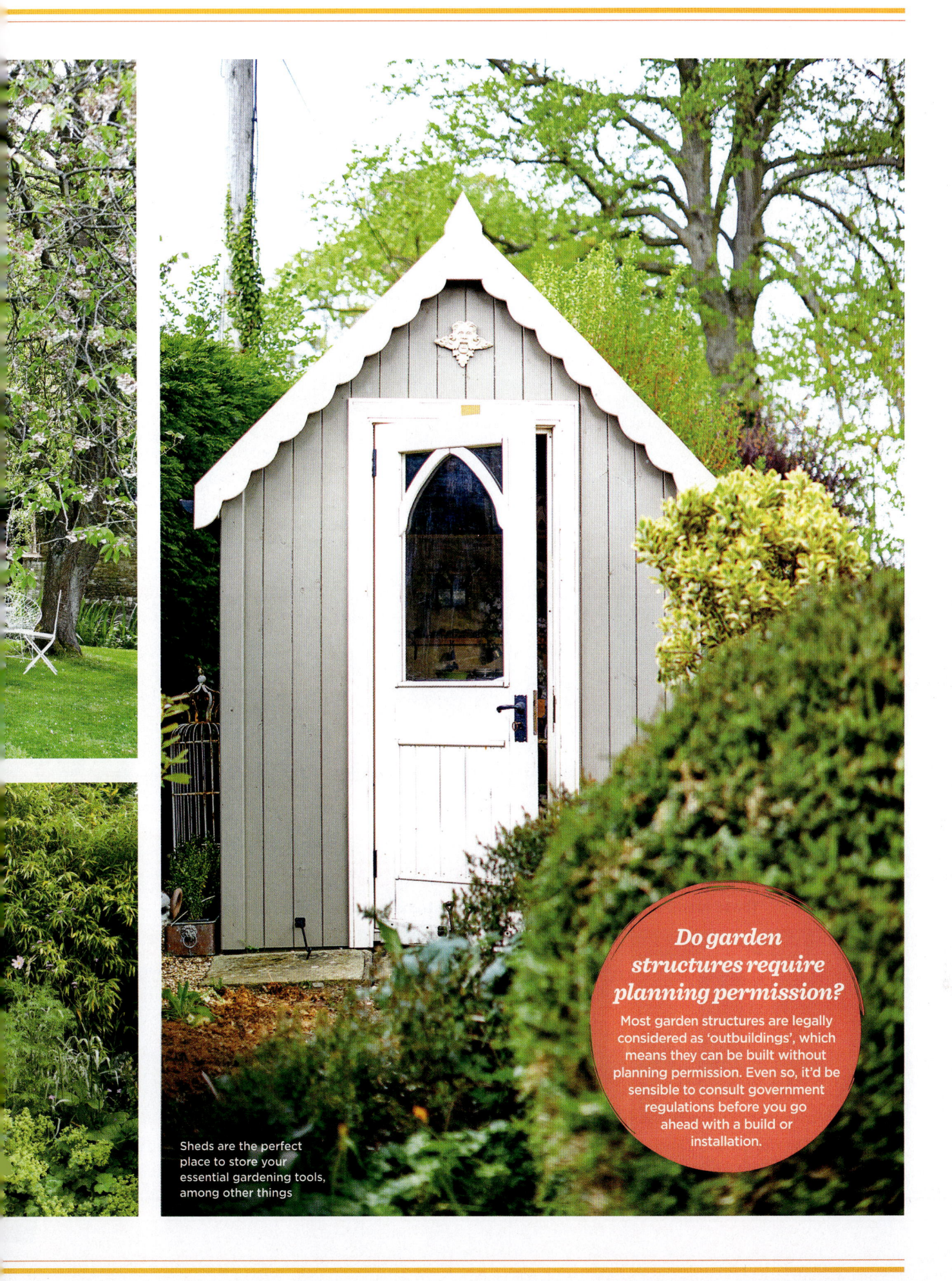

Sheds are the perfect place to store your essential gardening tools, among other things

Do garden structures require planning permission?

Most garden structures are legally considered as 'outbuildings', which means they can be built without planning permission. Even so, it'd be sensible to consult government regulations before you go ahead with a build or installation.

TRANSFORM YOUR GARDEN ON A BUDGET | 89

Pergolas offer a great space for hosting and outdoor dining

3 of the best... GARDEN STRUCTURES

These ready-made structures will instantly transform your outdoor space

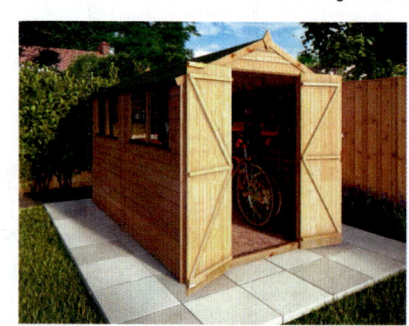

10 x 6 Overlap Double Door Apex Wooden Shed
£599.99, WWW.WALTONS.CO.UK

The Clara Log Cabin
£3,773.99, WWW.TIGERSHEDS.COM

Forest Garden Square Pergola
£630, WWW.DIY.COM

BUYER'S GUIDE TO GARDEN STRUCTURES

For the latest guidance, visit: planningportal.co.uk/permission/common-projects/outbuildings/planning-permission

Why not customise your shed for different uses?

verandahs, awnings and other aspirational add-ons. Some higher-end or bespoke examples are crafted to resemble specific traditional outdoor buildings, such as a Japanese tea house or North American log cabin.

As well as beckoning in sunlight, a summerhouse needs to keep out the rain. A tile-effect roof will typically provide good waterproofness in the long term, while roofing felt is a cheaper but less robust option. Investing in a summerhouse with high-quality roofing will pay dividends over long, happy years in the garden.

WHAT MAKES THE PERFECT SUMMERHOUSE?

The ideal layout for your summerhouse will depend on how you wish to use it. You'll certainly need space for a sofa or comfy chairs, and probably a table too. Beyond these essentials, you can add all sorts of items, from desks and televisions to hot tubs and exercise equipment. A summerhouse can be a chillout zone, office, creative space, or pretty much whatever you want it to be. Before buying one, check the dimensions and floor plan, and sketch out a scale drawing to show how your belongings would fit into the space.

Placement of a summerhouse will colour how it plays into the garden. Most households choose to position these structures near a boundary, as this avoids creating 'dead space' behind the summerhouse. If you would like the structure to get plenty of sunlight, it'd be ideal for its front side to be south-facing, or east-facing to catch the morning light. Also consider the view from your summerhouse's doors and windows. Which aspects of your home and garden will you gaze upon from this outdoor sanctuary?

Summerhouses are expensive compared to other types of garden structure, so budget will likely factor heavily into your buying decision. You're looking at an outlay between £500 and £1,000s, before you even start to furnish the summerhouse.

PERGOLAS, ARCHES AND ARBOURS

Partially open garden structures including pergolas, arbours and arches can bring you closer to your prized plants. These spaces often provide seating or shelter, while their beams or lattices can become home to beautiful climbers like wisteria, honeysuckle, clematis and climbing roses.

A pergola is an open-sided garden structure supported by vertical beams, sometimes featuring a permanent or retractable 'roof'. Various types are available from online retailers, including flat-packed kits or pre-assembled models that can be easily installed on decking or secured into the ground.

When deciding which pergola to buy, consider your outdoor design scheme as a whole. Traditional pergolas made from wood tend to go well with English country gardens or formal rose gardens, while contemporary designs made from materials such as aluminium and steel can look great with immaculate lawns or Mediterranean planting.

Garden arches are quite similar to pergolas, but have a smaller footprint and – usually – an arched top. Most are typically made from wood or metal, with plenty of surfaces that climbing plants can grow around.

Arbours combine an arch or roof with standing room or seating, and usually feature trellised sides. When choosing an arbour, consider where it will be placed. Some are designed to be situated in corners, creating a perfect sheltered nook within the garden.

A NATURAL FIT FOR YOUR GARDEN

Pergolas, arches and arbours are at their best when they serve plants, as well as people. These structures sprung up in scores of European formal gardens through the 19th and early 20th centuries, partly because their trellised features provided an ideal support for climbing roses, which had been popularised by trendsetters including Joséphine de Beauharnais, Queen of Italy (1763-1814).

If you wish to grow climbers on your garden structure – and we strongly suggest you do – choose a structure with trellising, which gives the plants plenty of purchase. Climbing plants will require adequate sunlight, according to their species.

Finally, think carefully about how each structure will fit into your garden design. Pergolas and arches can guide the eye and the feet through a garden, breaking up the space into distinct sections. Arbours are a resting place and a vantage point, immersed in beauty.

FEATURE PETE WISE

TRANSFORM YOUR GARDEN ON A BUDGET | 91

Get creative with GARDEN PAINT

Give your outdoor space a facelift using striking paint treatments

Although the go-to paints for outdoor spaces has often been white, as a nation we're becoming more adventurous with our paint choices, embracing bolder colours.

'Maintaining and refreshing exterior masonry and woodwork not only protects the surfaces but it is a great way of creating an impression, particularly if you embrace colour,' says Helen Shaw at Benjamin Moore. 'Choosing the right paint for your garden can be complicated, as there are a range of surfaces needing different finishes. Happily, there's an exterior paint to suit every type of surface and choosing a bolder colour is a great way of creating a standout look or transforming outdoor features.'

1 LIVEN UP A FENCE

Give a dull and uninspiring boundary fence a colour boost by painting it a bold shade. Cool blues and greys help to create a calm feeling and mirror the colour of the sky to create a sense of openness. You can also use bright colours to lighten shady areas of the garden.

TYPES OF OUTDOOR PAINT

LIMEWASH
Ideal for porous surfaces like brick, stone or plaster. It needs renewing about every five years.

MASONRY PAINT
Great for refreshing render, this comes in a good range of colours. Opt for a textured finish if you need to disguise surface cracks.

GLOSS/EGGSHELL
There is a wide range of wood paint available, but make sure you prep wood first with a primer for the best finish.

METAL PAINT
This is a hardwearing product as it's used to protect railings and gates. Metal usually requires priming before painting, but some brands like Hammerite can be applied directly.

CHALK PAINT
Using Annie Sloan's Chalk Paint is an easy way to freshen up tired furniture or brickwork. Use water resistant UV protective Chalk Paint Lacquer after to seal it.

Priddy Pools royal exterior paint, Protek

SPRUCE UP THE SHED

2 Choosing the best colour for your garden shed will depend on its location and whether you want the structure to blend in or stand out. Soft greens and blues are perfect if you want the shed to merge in with foliage or if you want it be a focal point, opt for a bold colour that complements your planting scheme.

GET CREATIVE WITH GARDEN PAINT

Wall in Linen Wash; window in Loft White intelligent exterior eggshell, Little Greene

5 TIPS FOR USING PAINT IN YOUR GARDEN

1 Revive hard landscaping such as walls, fences and decking. A fresh coat of vibrant paint will revamp jaded surfaces. It can take your outdoor space up a level and completely change the feel by adding a smart contemporary touch.

2 Create interest with paint by using it to transform a dull space. If you're nervous about using bold colours on large areas like fencing, restrict it to smaller surfaces like furniture, planters and garden accessories instead.

3 Stick to a colour theme for the best results. Take an accent colour like a pretty shade of pink that you can then co-ordinate with matching blooms. Avoid using too many colours as this will look chaotic and won't create a restful environment.

4 Spend time prepping properly. Fail to prepare and before long you could end up having to do it all over again. Make sure surfaces are clean, wood is lightly sanded and any rotten timber removed and replaced before you start. Paints and varnishes sit on the surface of the wood and create a protective layer. When it's time to reapply you will need to sand them again before you start.

5 Check the weather before starting your painting project. You want to avoid painting when it's raining (or if rain is due). Equally, painting in hot temperatures can make the job harder as the paint dries too quickly and paintbrushes get clogged up easily.

5 KEEP IT MUTED
Sometimes toning things down can have just as much impact as going bold. Keeping to a neutral palette of off-white, pale grey and soft cream on exterior walls, woodwork and outdoor furniture creates an easy-to-achieve look that's elegant and low key.

Wall painted in Tuscan Red intelligent masonry paint; table legs and plant pot painted in Grey Teal intelligent exterior eggshell, Little Greene

'CHOOSE PAINT COLOURS THAT WILL COMPLEMENT YOUR PLANTS, WHETHER BOLD OR MUTED'

3 CREATE A LUXE HOLIDAY FEEL
Dusky shades of terracotta and coral add a Tuscan vibe to the garden and will create a holiday feeling every time you eat outdoors. Tuscan Red is an earth tone based on naturally occurring red ochre pigment that adds a classical touch. Pair it with cool grey and off-white to complement the look.

4 PERK UP A CHAIR
If furniture has weathered over time, it's easily spruced up with a coat of paint. Just one colourful piece of furniture in a vibrant shade can enliven a garden. Use sealant on furniture that will be left outdoors to prolong your handiwork.

Give new life to old furniture with a lick of exterior paint, M&L Paints

TRANSFORM YOUR GARDEN ON A BUDGET | 93

6 ADD A SIGNATURE WALL

Take this interior trend outside to add impact to your garden decor and create the feel of an al fresco living room. A gorgeous shade of mustard yellow will work in both a sunny and a shady spot. Pick out window and door frames with darker hues in shades of charcoal or blue-black to add to the contemporary look.

Back wall painted in Yellow Pink; right wall painted in Scree intelligent masonry paint, Little Greene

7 GO FOR DARK TONES

As surprising as it may sound, painting your fence a dark recessive shade such as black or grey can help to make the garden feel bigger and less enclosed. Eyes tend not to register dark colours as well, so will focus on plants and greenery instead, blurring the boundary lines.

Try Black Matt exterior wood paint, Cuprinol

'AS YOU WOULD INDOORS, USE TESTER POTS TO SEE HOW THE COLOUR LOOKS OUTSIDE – TRY PAINTING ON A PIECE OF BOARD'

SPEEDY PAINT MAKEOVERS
Give tired garden furniture and planters a fresh new look

Mid Green Superdec, Sadolin

Natural Slate Garden Colour Matt, Wickes

Dazzling Yellow Garden Shades paint, Cuprinol

SWITCH UP A TABLE
Transform an old table into a colourful raised planter. Simply remove the legs and turn the tabletop upside down to give an enclosed area for soil and plants. Refix the legs and paint a punchy paint colour. Prep the surface properly before painting.

REVAMP A PLANTER
Give a weathered timber planter a new lease of life by painting it a standout colour. Shades like charcoal, slate and graphite grey add a modern touch. The dark tones make the perfect background to contrast with colourful flowers and foliage.

UPCYCLE A PALLET
Make use of a discarded pallet by turning it into a low table, adding castors underneath so that it can be wheeled around. Paint the wood a bold accent colour that will create a focal point and use a specialist exterior wood paint to withstand the weather.

★ ON SALE NOW! ★

Create your dream home without breaking the bank

In this brand-new bookazine from the makers of Style at Home magazine, we share some of our best tips, tricks, advice and inspiration to help you update your house for less

Ordering is easy. Go online at:

WWW.MAGAZINESDIRECT.COM

Or get it from selected supermarkets & newsagents

FUTURE

Paint a tiered HERB PLANTER

Revamp tired-looking timber with a bold paint treatment that will transform a plain planter into a unique and colourful piece

Wooden garden planters get faded and weather-worn after being outdoors in all seasons. Painting with a quality exterior paint will add colour and protect wood from the elements, but why not have some fun too and create your own unique piece by using paint to create different patterns and effects?

YOU WILL NEED
✱ **Paintbrushes** ✱ **Wooden vertical planter** ✱ **Painter's tape** ✱ **Protek Royal Exterior paint (assorted shades)** ✱ **Protek Royal Metallic paint in Copper**

1 SORT THE BASE FIRST
Paint the legs of your planter with two coats of paint in your chosen colour and allow to dry thoroughly.

2 MAKE DIAGONAL SHAPES
Use painter's tape to mask off diagonal lines across each of the wooden troughs. Make sure the diagonal lines go in alternate directions on each of the trough's layers. Press the tape firmly against the wood to ensure the paint won't bleed through.

3 APPLY THE FIRST TWO SHADES
Paint the top half of each trough using two coats of paint in a pale colour (we used Lime White and Pond Green) and allow the paint to dry thoroughly. Carefully remove the tape and reposition it over the edge of the layer you have just painted to ensure the two painted diagonals butt up together neatly. Press the tape down firmly to prevent bleed-through.

4 CHOOSE A CONTRAST COLOUR
Next, paint the bottom half of each trough with two coats of paint in a darker contrast colour (we used Faded Terracotta). Allow the paint to dry thoroughly, but do not remove the tape just yet.

5 PAINT LEAF SHAPES
Use paint in contrast colours to create different patterns on each of the troughs. Try painting a simple abstract leaf shape in a darker shade of Forest Green (shown on the top trough) repeating it randomly.

6 ADD METALLIC STRIPES
Create painted stripes by applying lengths of tape vertically at regular intervals on top of a paler painted section. Use a flat artist's brush to apply two coats of copper metallic paint to the unmasked areas (to create the striped effect shown on the second trough). Allow paint to dry.

7 CREATE AN ANIMAL PRINT EFFECT
Paint a fun leopard skin effect on another of the terracotta-painted sections. Use a small artist's brush to create the dark outline shape and once dry, paint inside the centre of each using copper metallic paint (shown on the third trough). Once all the painted areas are dry, carefully remove all of the tape from the different troughs and plant up with a selection of herbs.

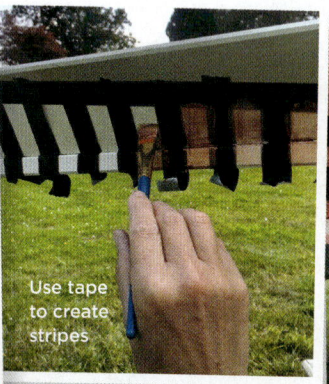

Press the tape firmly in place

Paint two contrasting shades

Go freehand with an artist's brush

Use tape to create stripes

Fill in with a copper shade

FEATURE AND PHOTOGRAPHS PROTEK

PAINT A TIERED HERB PLANTER

Troughs in Lime White, Pond Green, Faded Terracotta, Forest Green Royal Exterior paint, all Protek

IDEA TO STEAL
You can pick up vertical planters like this at garden centres – the wooden ladder planter at B&Q is similar

'FILL EACH TROUGH WITH COMPOST AND THEN PLANT IT UP WITH YOUR CHOSEN HERBS'

TRANSFORM YOUR GARDEN ON A BUDGET | 97

'We now have

GORGEOUS GREENERY
'Lavender and foliage spills out of the planters and softens hard edges'

MIX AND MATCH
'We combined natural timber fence panels with some painted a dark grey, which adds interest and makes the white seating really pop out'

IDEA TO STEAL
Horizontal slatted fencing is ideal for training climbing plants

COME ON IN!

ABOUT ME I'm Mel Feely, and I live with my husband Lochlin, and our three teenagers, in a four-bedroom, 1990s house in Berkshire. We moved here in 2011.

THE CHALLENGE Our back garden was mostly paved with scruffy concrete slabs and there was an old pond, which we filled in for safety. The whole space was very overgrown and pretty uninviting, so we didn't really use it.

MY WISH LIST I wanted somewhere to relax and entertain outside. It had to be a laid-back family-friendly space that added something to our home, and wouldn't be outgrown in a few years. I wanted a modern look, with sunken-bench seating and easy to manage planting.

98 | TRANSFORM YOUR GARDEN ON A BUDGET

an EXTRA ROOM'

Keen to transform her neglected garden, Mel created a low-maintenance outdoor space that's great for relaxing

Revamping the back garden was way down the agenda when we moved here,' says Mel, 'as we were a busy family with some ambitious renovation plans for the house. We had a lawn in the front garden with space for the children to play, and we could eat outside there too, so the back garden wasn't a priority. It was mostly tatty concrete paving, plus some mature trees and shrubs, and lots of weeds. Apart from a bit of cutting back, we hardly ever went out there. Even so, we knew it definitely had potential, and we talked about making more of it one day.

Work on the house took several years, so by then I'd developed some really clear ideas for the back garden. I visualised a chilled, outside lounge that would be useful for years to come.

Planning the design
I have some interior design experience, so to save on the cost of a professional landscaper, I drew up my own plan. For inspiration, I looked online at contemporary, linear gardens made for relaxing, socialising and entertaining. The ones I liked best were in California or the Mediterranean; they had modern, sunken-bench seating, and easy-to-manage planting. I wanted decking, a firepit in the centre and a white-rendered wall for projecting a film onto in the evenings. The entire garden had to be cleared, but I knew I'd keep the amazing palm tree in one corner, which looks quite exotic, and I left a tall photinia shrub, and a dark-leafed plum tree as well.

The project begins
Our trusted builder carried out the skilled work, including levelling the plot and building the seating, but to save money, Lochlin and I pitched in as much as we could. We helped clear the site and put up fencing. I salvaged the rose bushes and lavender, which I replanted in the

TRANSFORM YOUR GARDEN ON A BUDGET | 99

IDEA TO STEAL
Creating different levels with decking and paving adds interest

CLEAN LINES
'I designed the multi-level seating – it's really versatile. Everyone can sit around the fire and chat or watch a film on the screen'

Do it! PAINT A FENCE

✱ Painting a fence protects and extends the life of the panels, and introduces outdoor colour.
✱ Wait for dry, warm weather, then cut back or cover nearby plants, and protect walls and paving with tarpaulins.
✱ Remove moss, dirt and old paint with a stiff brush. Use warm, soapy water if necessary, but let it dry completely before painting.
✱ Some, but not all, garden fence paints require a primer, so allow for this to dry before painting. Use a brush or roller and work in the same direction as the grain, and from the top down. If the paint is suitable and there is no wind, try a spray gun for speed. One coat should suffice, but apply a second if needed once it is dry.

'LEAVING SOME TREES WAS A GOOD IDEA – THEY HELPED GIVE THE NEW GARDEN A STRUCTURED, MORE ESTABLISHED FEEL'

BOLD FEATURE
'The decking was cleverly cut around our photinia shrub'

100 | TRANSFORM YOUR GARDEN ON A BUDGET

'WE NOW HAVE AN EXTRA ROOM'

front garden, and then we broke up the old paving. The seating was constructed first, then the flower beds and the cinema wall. We tested our projector indoors to get the correct image size and distance from the wall, and to work out where to fix an outdoor socket.

Next came the decking. We chose timber as it's more economical, and painted it ourselves. All the old paving rubble went underneath it, saving us money as we didn't need a skip. Watching the seating and structures taking shape was really exciting as I could finally see the design coming together.

Finishing off
With the features in place, next on the list was planting. I chose potted perennials in pinks and mauves, such as hydrangeas and campanulas that are easy to look after, plus ferns, grasses and lavender.

I didn't have much experience with plants, so it's been a learning curve. There's a small patch of artificial grass, which isn't my favourite thing, but it was all about easy maintenance. It never needs mowing, plus it's clean, child and pet-friendly and always looks perfect!

Time to relax
The garden definitely works as an extension of our home. It's an afternoon suntrap, and a lovely spot for a morning coffee, or just somewhere to sit and read. If we're entertaining in the evening, the adults chill and chat around the firepit, while the children sit on beanbags for a film. Everyone loves it!'

COLOUR CODE
'A tight palette for flowers and matching containers creates a strong statement'

HANDY STORAGE
'Our new Screwfix shed is screened from some angles by slatted fencing, and it's painted dark grey so that it almost disappears'

FEATURE ANNABELLE GRUNDY PHOTOGRAPHS COLIN POOLE

TRANSFORM YOUR GARDEN ON A BUDGET | 101

How to know whether a heater can be kept outdoors

Check the IP rating before permanently installing an outdoor heater. There are two numbers in a product's ingress protection (IP) rating. The first indicates resilience against dust (from 1 to 6), while the second indicates resistance to water (1 to 9). So, a heater rated IP69 would have the highest ratable protection. For permanent outdoor use, look for a heater with a water resistance rating of IPX5 or higher.

Prolong your time outdoors with the right type of garden heating

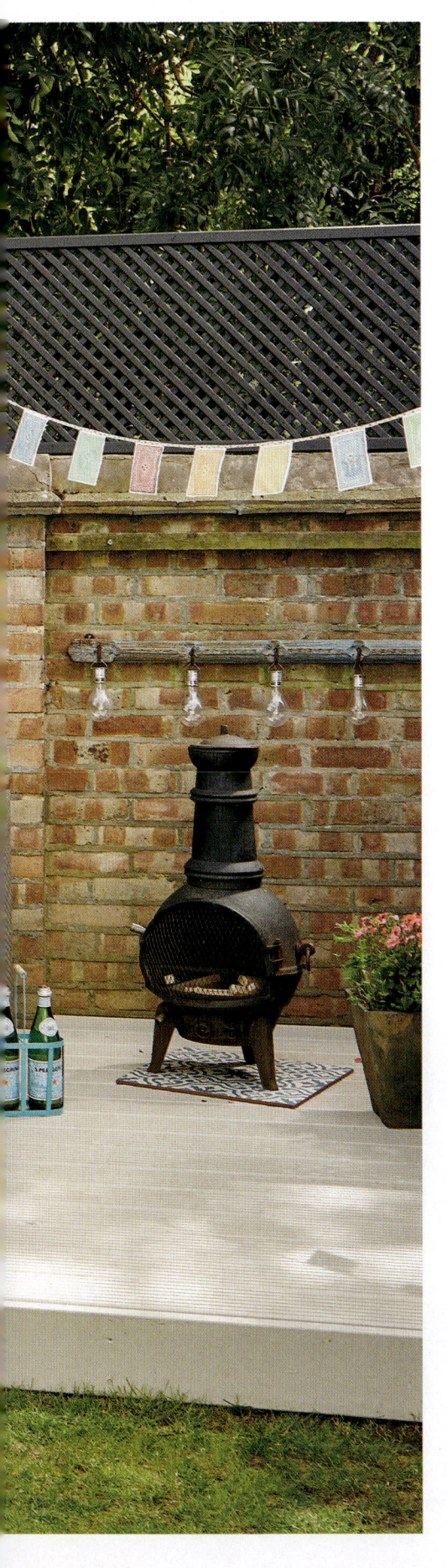

Buyer's guide to GARDEN HEATING

The warm heart of your garden glow-up

Effective garden heating is an investment in outdoor livability. As balmy evenings give way to night, or even during cooler summer days, we gravitate towards sources of warmth and light. Often, that means retreating indoors – but it doesn't have to.

Electric or gas-fuelled patio heaters, wood-burning fire pits and chimeneas all have the warming power to keep garden get-togethers or family moments glowing deeper into the night, and later into the year. These lifestyle-enhancing devices will naturally become a focal point whenever you use them, so it's well worthwhile to find a model that perfectly suits the design scheme and heating requirements of your outdoor space.

FREE-STANDING HEATERS

Setting up a free-standing patio heater is a reliable, straightforward way to add warmth to an outdoor space. These upright heaters can be positioned right at the heart of your patio, or wherever they're needed most, to provide a cosy hotspot for everyone to gather around.

All free-standing patio heaters give out warmth – but they use a few different energy sources to do it. Gas-fuelled freestanding patio heaters burn fuels such as butane or propane, much like a gas barbecue or camping stove does. They offer great flexibility, as there's no need to connect the heater to an electricity supply. However, you'll need to change or refill your butane or propane canister regularly to ensure the heater doesn't run out of fuel during use.

Electric free-standing patio heaters are powered by mains electricity and give off warmth via heating elements. If you intend to keep an electric free-standing in the same place permanently, then it'd make sense to get it hardwired to your household power supply by a qualified electrician. Or, for greater flexibility (and less expense), you can simply plug the heater into an outdoor power socket or extension cord, taking care to avoid unsafe contact with water.

Some smaller free-standing heaters are portable, with a handle at the top of the device that makes it easy to move from place to place. Larger models can sometimes be moved using in-built casters – but not during use.

Another point of difference is aesthetics. Freestanding heaters come in various styles, ranging from functional, contemporary towers to lamp- or lantern-like forms that bring a homelier feel to your outdoor space. Finishes range from chic chrome or black to bronze or copper. Think about how your chosen heater will play into your outdoor design scheme.

Of course, the level of heat matters too – you'll need enough power to comfortably heat a certain area. Look at specifications such as a heater's wattage and its BTU rating for a quick indication of the coverage provided. As a rule, you're aiming for roughly 20 BTUs per square foot of heated outdoor space.

WALL-MOUNTED HEATERS

There are upsides to installing a wall-mounted heater. Above all, you're saving on the valuable floor space that would be taken up by any model of freestanding heater, which will pay dividends if you're working with a smaller space.

Most mounted outdoor heaters are powered via a hardwired connection to your household electricity supply. You'll need to pay for professional installation, but in the long term you'll benefit from easy operation and freedom from trailing power cables. Plug-in mounted models are also available, which is good news for users who prioritise flexibility and lower up-front costs.

Like free-standing heaters, wall-mounted patio heaters vary in their

TRANSFORM YOUR GARDEN ON A BUDGET | 103

Chimeneas and table-top heaters can help warm a small area on a cold evening

104 | TRANSFORM YOUR GARDEN ON A BUDGET

BUYER'S GUIDE TO GARDEN HEATERS

3 of the best... GARDEN HEATERS
Hot picks from the most popular outdoor heating categories

Swan Column Patio Heater
£149.99,
WWW.SHOP.SWAN-BRAND.CO.UK

Terrace Pendant Electric Heater
£169,
WWW.KETTLER.CO.UK

El Clásico Chimenea
£109.95,
WWW.DIY.COM

heating power, which you can assess by looking at specifications including their wattage and BTU rating. In most cases, people will stand or sit further away from a wall-mounted heater than they would from a freestanding heater. So, you may benefit from choosing a relatively high-powered model.

THE RIGHT MOUNTED HEATER FOR YOUR SPACE
Placement of a mounted outdoor heater is key. Think about:

- Position: which area do you want the heater to cover?
- Stability: can the wall of your home or garden structure support the heater's weight?
- Power: how will the heater connect to electricity?
- Clearance: does your chosen placement leave enough clearance from surfaces and flammable items, based on the manufacturer's instructions?

In terms of design, mounted outdoor heaters are pretty homogenous. Most have a simple rectangular or oval-shaped design that delivers efficient heating, without making a style statement. If you're looking for a beautiful, head-turning design, you'd be better off buying a hanging, ceiling-mounted heater, provided that you have a sturdy garden structure that can accommodate one. Hanging heaters come in a relatively wide range of styles, from industrial-chic lamps to more basic, functional forms.

Where mounted heaters vary most significantly is in their features. High-performing models tend to offer useful extras, including timed heating and adjustable temperature settings. Some have remote control or smartphone operability, which comes in very handy when your heater is mounted above head height.

FIRE PITS AND CHIMENEAS
A wood-burning fire pit or chimenea brings spectacle and excitement to your outdoor space – as well as warmth.

Fire pits of various designs seem to have been used for heating, ritual and cookery throughout history. These have ranged from Dakota fire holes dug into the earth by the Očhéthi Šakówin peoples of North America, to off-the-shelf present day examples, which commonly take the form of a metal bowl supported by legs.

Bowl-shaped fire pits make a great focal point, and they burn wood efficiently. However, there are some eye-catching alternative fire pit designs available too, including rectangular and barrel-shaped models. Some premium lifestyle brands offer fire pits built into a table under safety glass, placing a display of dancing flames right into the midst of your dinner guests.

Whatever form you choose, any good fire pit will have a few key attributes. It should have sides steep enough to shelter fuel from the elements, so that it can catch light and stay lit. The material will conduct heat as much as you need it to – whether that means strongly via metal, or at a gentler, child-safe level through a material with lower heat conductivity, such as concrete or brick. And above all, it should be beautiful.

Chimeneas are another traditional heating device that can bring a rustic glow to your garden. These freestanding stoves were first developed in early modern Spain and Mexico, and can be identified by their open stove door and tall, vertical chimney. Classically, chimeneas are made of clay, although some contemporary designs are constructed from other materials such as cast iron or steel. Most of the warmth from a chimenea is focused forwards – which is perfect for thoroughly heating a small area.

Many fire pits and chimeneas use wood fuels such as hardwood logs or briquettes. Burning wood adds a timeless ambience and aroma to an outdoor space – so long as you're successful in getting the fuel lit. If the task of lighting a fire leaves you cold, a gas-fuelled fire pit or chimenea could be the ideal convenient alternative.

FEATURE PETE WISE

TRANSFORM YOUR GARDEN ON A BUDGET | 105

FACT FILE

✶ **THE DETAILS** Antony Watkins, a garden designer, and Christopher Hutchings, a media lawyer, have filled their 18x14m back garden with palms and exotic plants in a dynamic range of colours that peak in late summer.

✶ **THE CHALLENGE** The heavy clay soil waterlogs, making it unsuitable for growing palms, so it was supplemented with around 15 huge bags of topsoil, as well as many bags of grit to further improve drainage.

✶ **THE PLAN** To tame the 3m fall from the house to the back fence with a sloping path that brings the planting to eye level before arriving at an area for outdoor eating and cooking.

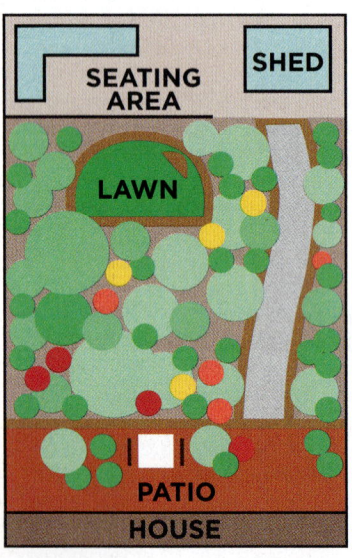

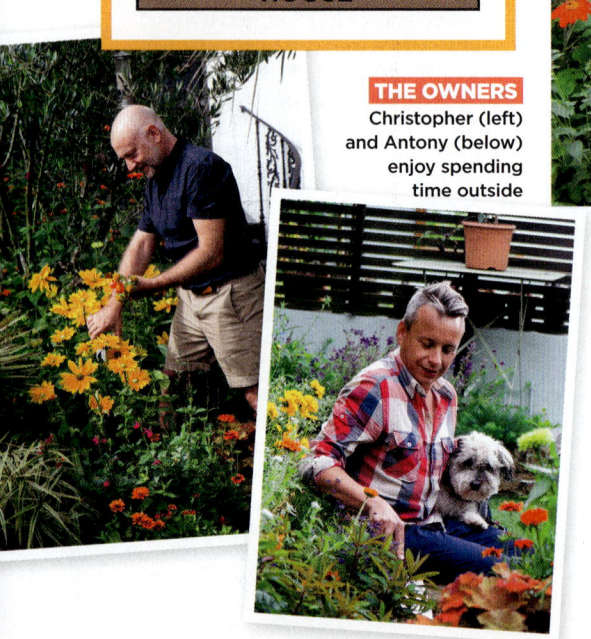

TROPICAL TOWN
The garden is planted with hot coloured perennials, olive and palm trees

THE OWNERS
Christopher (left) and Antony (below) enjoy spending time outside

Downtown
OASIS

Owners Antony and Christopher have turned a traditional town garden into a tropical paradise

106 | TRANSFORM YOUR GARDEN ON A BUDGET

DOWNTOWN OASIS

When we first went house hunting, our approach was somewhat different to the norm because it was not the interior that mattered most, but what was beyond.

It was the back garden that we always asked to see first – often to the amusement of both vendors and estate agents. We found the 1880s detached house 15 years ago down a quiet west London street. We nearly didn't view it because the online plan wrongly showed the garden as north-facing, when in fact it faces south.

The plot turned out to be both an ideal size and not overlooked, a rare find in London. And when we saw that the garden backs directly onto allotments, we decided there and then to make it our home.

In the decade since, we've jointly created a tropical oasis with a strong framework of yuccas, bamboos, cannas, olives and cacti. The giant torch cactus is a major talking point among the collection of pots on the tiled terrace.

Tropical vibes

There are also a number of evergreen palms, ranging from the smaller Blue Fan Palm to a Jelly Palm, and Chusan palm that has settled in so happily that it almost brushes our bedroom window. Then, woven through the permanent planting, is a tapestry of late-flowering perennials and annuals. We chose hot-coloured flowers that are mostly sourced from Chiltern Seeds, who have a great range.

Each year, we grow new plants from seed, and experiment with planting

SLICE OF PARADISE
The bold shades of Tithonia, Canna and Zinnia lends a tropical feel to the seating area

TORCH CACTUS
Echinopsis spachiana is a prickly talking point

combinations that break up the space into a series of linked, miniature gardens.

Star performers

Our colour palette focuses on bright colours, using different varieties of zinnias, rudbeckias and verbenas blended among clumps of tall orange Mexican sunflowers that the bees love. We're not trying to mimic a jungle – it's more urban exotic as we call it! We grow plenty of our plants from seed in a greenhouse on the allotment. The allotment was one of the key factors in choosing to live here because it allows us to grow everything ourselves – flowers and also lots of veg.

The long view

When you stand on the balcony outside our living room, at the top of an iron staircase that leads down to the garden, it is hard to imagine the original garden. Back then, the view was an untidy rectangle of grass with a straight, tiled path leading from front to back, ending by a diseased plum and old cherry tree. At the very back, the level dropped away to a gate that opens out onto an alley leading to the allotment entrance.

At first, all we did was to clear plenty of ivy, some untidy shrubs and the tree. Then, for the first couple of years we tried out possible designs on the old lawn while we got to know the site, and how the sun moved around, in order to arrive at the best layout.

Entertaining space

Near the top of our wish list was an area for entertaining, with permanent seating, a good barbecue and cooking area. We also wanted a cabin which, while

108 | TRANSFORM YOUR GARDEN ON A BUDGET

DOWNTOWN OASIS

HIGHWAY TO HEAVEN
The winding path takes you past *Chamaerops humilis*, *Erigeron karvinskianus* and *Agapanthus*

'WE LOVE ARCHITECTURAL PLANTS – THEY FORM THE BACKBONE OF THE GARDEN, GIVING GREENERY THROUGHOUT THE YEAR'

providing a focal point to glimpse through the planting, also stores bikes and garden furniture.

We drew up various designs before settling on a sunken, S-shaped path to create the feeling of a journey from the house to this area.

With a fall of 3m from the patio to the end fence, we decided to lower the entire path, rather than have steps at the far end. This allows you to walk down the garden with most planting raised up closer to eye level, rather than at foot level. So we started excavating out the soil but it became clear that the path would need retaining walls. We sourced some reclaimed London stock bricks which have an aged appearance that is in keeping with the surrounding houses.

A builder did the walls for us, as well as fixing trellis to the boundary walls. This creates more privacy, but without either blocking or stealing light from our neighbours. They also installed a contemporary wooden screen two-thirds of the way down, dividing off the entertainment area.

Going in circles

We decided on a circular-shaped lawn in the end after trying out several alternatives. This allows the eye to keep moving, fooling it into thinking the dimensions are greater.

Mowing the circular lawn proved difficult as the edges looked unkempt, so we replaced it with artificial grass which helps minimise the upkeep.

This is a garden that is really lived in, enjoyed, and shared with our friends and family. Yes, it was hard work, but it's a source of huge pleasure to us.

3 of the best... BRIGHT COMBINATIONS

A pastiche of fiery tones with the large paddle-shaped leaves of *Canna* 'Durban' alongside *Lobelia cardinalis* and *Zinnia* 'Benary's Giant Scarlet'.

An eye-catching mix of golden *Rudbeckia hirta* 'Irish Eyes' and *Zinnias* with red *Gaillardias* and shocking pink *Salvia greggii*.

A bark chipping path is edged in golden *Coreopsis grandiflora* 'Golden Globe', *Euphorbia*, blue *Brachyscome* and the pink succulent *Lampranthus cooperi*.

WORDS AND PHOTOGRAPHS NICOLA STOCKEN

TRANSFORM YOUR GARDEN ON A BUDGET | 109

365 days of COLOUR

Garden designer Tabi Jackson Gee shares the easy tricks garden designers use to get colour into gardens – all year round

Leave hydrangea flowerheads on to see you from summer to winter

110 | TRANSFORM YOUR GARDEN ON A BUDGET

365 DAYS OF COLOUR

With changing climates and lifestyles, many of us are expecting more from our gardens than ever before. From wintry fireside gatherings to spring al fresco lunches, they need to work harder to look good all year round. With that comes a new set of gardening jobs to think about, as well as new plants to acquaint yourself with. But, never fear, we have rounded up a whole host of tips to make this stress free – and none should add much to your to-do list, either. This is about achieving year-round colour without having to break the bank or spend hours in the garden every day.

We're used to gardens being a summer thing, but we need to consider the rest of the year too. How do you design a garden that looks alive, and full with colour all year round? From evergreen shrubs to seasonal bulbs, here, we've outlined the many ways you can have a colourful garden from January to December.

GETTING STARTED
When doing anything in your garden, it's best to start with the essentials. There are certain conditions that need to be observed and noted over time, in order for us to get the most out of our gardens. The key ones are: light, weather conditions, temperature and soil type.

Next, be realistic about how much maintenance you can (and want to) do. For your garden to thrive and with a succession of colour all through the year, you will probably need to put aside a couple of hours a week in spring/summer to take care of it. If you have less time, choose fewer, bigger plants that have long seasons of interest. When you've made a note of all of these factors, it's time to start planning your garden.

---

3 of the best... FOR SPRING
Easy to grow and sure to welcome in the new season beautifully

TULIPA 'PRINSES IRENE'

IRIS RETICULATA

HELLEBORUS X HYBRIDUS HARVINGTON RED

Diverse planting is good for soil health as well as colour

FEATURE TABI JACKSON GEE PHOTOGRAPHS ALAMY, FUTURECONTENTHUB.COM

TRANSFORM YOUR GARDEN ON A BUDGET | 111

Take a piece of paper and jot down existing plants, where the sun goes throughout the day, where any wet patches or dry patches are – and get ready to start scheming.

HOW TO PLAN

It may be useful to draw up a calendar when planning your year of colour, then you can start to plot into that calendar which plants you like and research when they will flower. If you are particularly fond of spring, for example, then maybe you want to go big on cherries and other spring-blossoming trees, as well as bulbs such as narcissus, tulips and alliums.

You'll notice when you do this where some plants cross over, either when their foliage starts growing or flowers bloom. The key is to think about the succession of the plants in your garden – they will be appearing and flourishing and dying back over different periods, so try to make sure there are lots of overlapping plants grouped together.

CHOOSING YOUR PLANTS

Consider what style of planting you like. You don't have to stick to one style – cottage garden, Mediterranean or prairie planting, for instance – but if you have an idea of which direction you're going in creatively, then it will help you narrow down which plants to use.

The real key to choosing plants that will thrive in your garden ultimately lies in finding the right plants for the right place. Now that you've worked out where the shade, sun and wet and dry areas of your garden are, this will help you pick what plants will work where in your space.

When selecting plants a great tip that designers use is to work from the biggest to the smallest. For instance, begin by deciding which plants are going to form the structural elements of the garden. These are usually shrubs or trees that are either evergreen or have year-round interest, through blossom, winter berries or beautiful bark.

Next, it's the smaller seasonal plants that will create interest at different stages in the year, then finally the plants that are the supporting acts, such as clumps of hardy geraniums or evergreen grasses, which will be the reliable foundations of your scheme.

CREATE A COLOUR SCHEME

There are so many colours you can fit into a garden. Often when I show clients a planting moodboard they're taken aback and think I've picked out too many shades or clashing colours, but what you have to remember is that most plants only flower for a few weeks at a time.

Cool down a colour scheme with silvery foliage plants, such as Stachys byzantina *'Silver Carpet'*

Plants in containers can be switched in and out throughout the year

---

3 of the best... FOR SUMMER
Go for prolific flowerers which will give you a long season of blooms

GERANIUM ORION

COSMOS

NEPETA RACEMOSA 'WALKER'S LOW'

---

112 | TRANSFORM YOUR GARDEN ON A BUDGET

365 DAYS OF COLOUR

When choosing a colour scheme, it's also important to consider the texture, shape, height, form and movement of the planting. These are the less obvious features of our plants that can all contribute to year-round interest. From soft silky grasses to spiky eryngiums and neat mounds of pittosporum, these elements all add up to make a beautiful garden when carefully thought through.

USING EVERGREENS
Evergreen shrubs, as well as evergreen spreading ground-cover plants, are particularly valuable for giving interest when there's not much else going on.

I often use pittosporum in gardens as it's a good alternative to box. Additionally, hebes, daphnes, choisyas and viburnum are all brilliant shrubs as they flower at different times in the year and can grow to a good size in a relatively short period of time. Do check when buying shrubs that your chosen variety is actually evergreen. For instance, some viburnums are deciduous.

LONG-FLOWERING PLANTS
Any scheme, of any size, should have reliable plants in it. Hardy geraniums spring to mind here, as do salvias, sanguisorbas, cosmos, erigeron and heucheras. All these plants are fairly tough and not especially fussy about their exact conditions, and they will flower for months at a time.

Allow yourself time to deadhead to keep plants flowering reliably. Choose

If you like multi-coloured schemes go for an array of bright shades

TRANSFORM YOUR GARDEN ON A BUDGET | 113

Trees and shrubs are vital for creating a backbone for your planting scheme

3 of the best...
FOR AUTUMN
The floral fun doesn't stop in autumn with these late bloomers

NERINE BOWDENII

EURYBIA X HERVEYI

HELENIUM AUTUMNALE

two dates a year when you'll do a big day of general maintenance. Then do little bits here and there as time allows throughout the growing season.

SHRUBBY ADDITIONS
Most shrubs only need pruning and mulching once a year. Just make sure you look up which variety you have as some shrubs enjoy being cut back on old wood, some on new wood, most directly after they've finished flowering.

One of the most popular shrubs is the hydrangea, whose large flowerheads start to form in spring and give way to months of colour as summer gets going. Leave the dried hydrangea blooms on over winter to protect new growth from frost, they also help maintain the shrub's shape.

Another winner is the cornus (dogwood), many varieties of which have deep red or orange stems that shine in a winter garden.

BULB MATTERS RIGHT
No garden is complete without bulbs. They're the easiest plants to look after, requiring little attention after their initial planting, and they bring colour to our gardens at a time when not much else is going on. What's more, there are so many colours to choose from here that you can go to town! Choosing bulbs that repeat or naturalise (tulips don't but most other bulbs do) will mean you can plant one year and then let the bulbs do their thing for years after.

WINTER INTEREST
Swaying ornamental grasses are one of my favourite plants to use in a scheme, and they require very little maintenance.

365 DAYS OF COLOUR

3 of the best... FOR WINTER
The winter garden can sparkle with foliage colour and bright stems

CORNUS ALBA 'SIBIRICA'

EDGEWORTHIA CHRYSANTHA

CROCUS SUBLIMIS 'TRICOLOR'

Choose acers for a backdrop of autumn colour

Seedheads look stunning in a frost or in low sun during winter months

Balance the softness of these with more architectural-shaped plants like alliums or phlomis for a contrasted look that works almost all year round.

Leave allium seedheads on after they've gone over, they look stunning in a frost or in the late low sun of a winter's afternoon, sparkling in the landscape. Equally phlomis, erygiums, sanguisorbas, sedums, Teasels and many more plants can be left in borders after they've 'gone over' to be enjoyed all through the winter. Some will retain some colour, others will fade but still give you shadows and shapes within your border that would otherwise be missing during the colder darker months. Just make sure you cut them back in early spring to allow space for new growth.

TRANSFORM YOUR GARDEN ON A BUDGET | 115

January
START THE YEAR

Now is the time to plan ahead. Check last season's garden photos, noting any gaps in the borders. Could there be more structure, colour or interest?

Star of the month

HAMAMELIS 'DIANE'
This striking witch hazel is at its peak, pumping its powerful spicy perfume around the January garden. It has spidery flowers on bare stems in a stunning deep red.
H3m

GARDENING CALENDAR

Seasonal container

Review your garden and cheer up January with some seasonal colour. A cordyline will give colour and structure as a centrepiece to a container in the dark days of winter. You will need a pot with a large hole in the bottom. Cover with crocks and multipurpose compost. Then you could fill the gaps around the base with trailing plants or spring flowering bulbs.

5 ESSENTIAL JOBS

1 **It's the perfect time to build paths and patios** while plants are still dormant, so organise landscaping jobs.

2 **There's still time to sow sweet peas** for flowers and scent in late May and through summer. Plant in peat-free multipurpose compost in tall pots or kitchen rolls and put somewhere warm. They'll flower earlier and make stronger plants.

3 **Deadhead winter-flowering pansies** weekly, to keep them blooming.

4 **Boring, maybe, but necessary** – clean pots and sharpen and oil tools for the new season.

5 **Check containers** in case they need watering – freezing weather can prevent them taking up water.

BEDS AND BORDERS

✱ Dig new borders if the soil isn't frozen or waterlogged. ✱ Prune climbing roses, removing the oldest stems at the base and tie in long shoots. ✱ Prune rose bush roses too. Clip away any dead branches, and a third to half of the top growth. Cut just 1cm above a bud. Aim for a 'vase' shape with space for air to circulate. ✱ Prune wisteria – cut side shoots back to 2-3 buds. They'll flower beautifully in spring. ✱ Help out your bulbs by adding a handful of bonemeal around emerging shoots, forking in lightly.

What to do in the ... VEG PATCH

✱ Design this season's veg plot, practising crop rotation to avoid build-up of pests and diseases. This means growing different kinds of veg in their own section, and changing them every year. Brassicas, such as cabbages, should go where peas and beans grew last year. Peas and beans should grow where you had potatoes, potatoes where you grew root vegetables and onions previously, and so on.

✱ Take time to review what crops were a success last year and what didn't work out. Plan what you're going to grow this year before ordering anything. Look through catalogues and visit the websites of specialist nurseries, and order veg seeds or plug (baby) plants for planting out later on.

Wildlife watch

✱ Wildlife needs our help in the worst winter weather. Keep bird feeders topped up with protein-rich foods such as lard and nuts. Remember to leave water for birds and other wildlife, especially in freezing weather.

✱ Avoid cutting back climbers like ivy now, which support overwintering birds and bees.

✱ In freezing weather, stop ice forming on ponds so that fish and frogs can get oxygen. Don't crack the ice, as this can send wildlife into shock – just float a rubber ball on the water's surface.

✱ Protect sweet pea seeds from mice, who love to eat them: cover pots with newspaper until seeds germinate.

FEATURE GERALDINE SWEENEY PHOTOGRAPHS ALAMY STOCK PHOTO

TRANSFORM YOUR GARDEN ON A BUDGET | 117

February
TENTATIVE SHOOTS

It's still winter, but small bulbs and early flowers are popping up in pots, borders and garden centres. On fine days, get ahead with your preparations for spring

5 ESSENTIAL JOBS

1 Prepare new lawns by weeding and digging over, treading level and raking. Let the soil settle before turfing later.

2 Start feeding your soil now, ready for the growing season. Organic feeds, such as fish, blood and bone and chicken manure pellets take around six weeks to release their nutrients. Fork into the soil around plants and water in.

3 Mow the lawn in mild weather if it begins to grow. Put the mower blade on the highest setting so you don't scalp the grass.

4 Winter heather will finish flowering; trim lightly with shears.

5 Prune clematis that blooms in summer (don't prune spring-flowering types, such as Montana). Cut back to knee-height, just above a pair of buds, and feed.

Star of the month
SNOWDROP (*GALANTHUS NIVALIS*)
These gems provide nectar in January and February. For best results, plant 'in the green' in spring, in leaf mould enriched soil, in semi-shade or shade, and they will naturalise.
H15cm

BEDS & BORDERS

✻ On warmer days, you'll notice the first stirrings of spring, so get ahead with your preparations in the garden before things get busy next month. ✻ You can start some proper gardening now, such as weeding and clearing your borders. ✻ Provided the soil is workable, and not waterlogged or frozen, you can dig new beds and borders and prepare sites for new lawns. ✻ While you're outside, enjoy the scents of early-spring shrubs, such as daphne, and the sight of bumblebees coming out of hibernation to feed on early flowers such as *Pulmonaria officinalis* (lungwort, above).

Wildlife watch

✻ Continue to attract birds by feeding them, to encourage them into the garden to snack on pests. Birds will be nesting soon; put up nest boxes now, so that they're a familiar part of the landscape. Choose a quiet part of the garden out of reach of cats.

✻ Aphids (greenfly) may appear on plants if there's a warm spell. No need to spray them yet – either remove by hand or, better still, allow hungry birds to hoover them up. Watch out for slugs on strawberry plants; protect them with fleece or hessian.

118 | TRANSFORM YOUR GARDEN ON A BUDGET

GARDENING CALENDAR

March
ALONG COMES SPRING...

It's time to head outside into the garden to tidy up the borders, and to buy new plants from the garden centre, guaranteed to put a spring in your step

Star of the month
CLEMATIS MACROPETALA
There's a clematis for every month of the year, and who could resist the early lavender-blue flowers of 'Virgin's Bower'. Plant it deeply in a sheltered spot against a trellis. H4m

Wildlife watch
✱ Create a mini pond to attract wildlife. Use a half barrel, a frost-proof terracotta pot or an old sink, blocking drainage holes with a waterproof sealant. Add a layer of gravel and stack bricks inside to support aquatic marginal plants. Fill with water and add a dwarf waterlily. Use rocks to act as stepping stones for wildlife. Top up the water with rainwater.

✱ Check for early whitefly on citrus and greenhouse plants. Symptoms include black mould on the leaves. Treat with an organic insecticide and wipe off the mould. Check for aphids on plants, too.

BEDS & BORDERS

✱ Now is the time to sow hardy annual seeds, such as sweet pea, nasturtium, nigella, calendula and cornflower, in pots or where they are to flower.

✱ More tender annual climbers can be started in a propagator; these have a twining habit and can quickly scale a support or scramble through a shrub. Try the cup and saucer vine (*Cobaea scandens*, above) or morning glory (*Ipomoea*).

5 ESSENTIAL JOBS

1 **Trim deciduous grasses before new leaves emerge.** *Miscanthus sinensis* can be cut back from mid-March to April.

2 **Apply a thick layer of mulch around shrubs.** This will keep weeds at bay and retain moisture.

3 **If the weather is fine, mow the grass.** For the first cut, raise the blade to its highest level.

4 **Take stock of borders**, plant new perennials and cut out the dead stems of dormant plants.

5 **Clean bird baths and bird tables** to reduce the risk of disease.

FEATURE GERALDINE SWEENEY PHOTOGRAPHS ALAMY STOCK PHOTO

TRANSFORM YOUR GARDEN ON A BUDGET | 119

April
THE GARDEN GETS BUSY

As the weather warms up and the garden comes to life, prepare for summer by sowing seeds for an abundance of flowers, fruit and veg later in the year

Wildlife watch

* Provide nesting boxes for garden birds, such as blue tits, and regularly clean and top up bird feeders with seed.
* Use a squirrel-proof bird feeder to prevent squirrels from stealing the food and don't let seed build up on the ground as it may attract rats.

BEDS & BORDERS

* Now is the time to divide up perennials, such as hostas, giving you more plants for the garden. Cut back the old shoots on penstemons to the base as long as there is new growth at the bottom of the plant.
* Sow sweet peas directly in the ground or plant out pot-grown seedlings and build wigwams of canes to support them, tying in the shoots as they grow.
* Train clematis up along a fence or trellis and tie in the shoots as they grow throughout the spring and summer.
* Remove the faded heads of tulips and daffodils but leave the foliage to die back naturally.

Star of the month
TULIPS
These bulb favourites are in their prime. Try *Tulipa* 'Flaming Parrot' for yellow and red striped petals or 'Pink Impression' (shown), with a subtle hint of bronze on pink. **H50cm**

5 ESSENTIAL JOBS

1 Repair bald patches of grass with lawn seed, keeping the soil moist while the seed germinates.

2 Sweep up your patio areas, removing any dead leaves or debris and use a pressure washer to clean the paving of mildew.

3 Weed borders and vegetable patches regularly as everything will start to grow quickly as the weather warms up – especially the weeds!

4 Tie in rambling and climbing roses as they grow to prevent unruly shoots sticking out.

5 Prepare the soil in your vegetable beds that haven't been used yet. Dig over and cover the soil with black plastic to keep it dry and warm in preparation for planting.

GARDENING CALENDAR

May
PREPARE FOR SUMMER...

As the risk of frost subsides this month, bedding plants are ready to add instant colour, while everything rapidly grows as the weather warms up – it's a busy time for the garden!

5 ESSENTIAL JOBS

1 Earth up potatoes, regularly as the foliage grows, keeping any tubers well covered.

2 Feed and cut your lawn regularly and make sure it is well watered in dry spells.

3 Keep on top of weeding, checking regularly for new growth.

4 Once all risk of frost has passed, put out summer bedding plants and make up hanging baskets.

5 Check hedges and long grass for wildlife before clipping or cutting. Don't use hedge trimmers during the nesting season.

Star of the month
SALLIUM 'MONT BLANC'
This impressive towering plant is great for adding height at the back of the border. Dense clusters of white flowers make this a real showstopper, plus the bees love them!
H2m

BEDS & BORDERS

✲ Give lavender a trim, removing old flowerheads and a couple of centimetres of growth. Don't cut back to the woody parts or new growth won't develop. Plant out pot-grown foxgloves (left) which flower from May to July. Bees love to feast on their nectar, and the towering blooms are iconic for a cottage-style scheme. ✲ *Geranium x oxonianum* 'Wargrave Pink' is great for filling borders and has a long flowering period, from May to October. ✲ After flowering, collect seeds from poppies, for next year.

Wildlife watch

✲ Cover carrots with horticultural fleece to prevent carrot fly infesting them.

✲ Surround soft fruit plants, such as raspberries, with netting to stop birds and squirrels eating the fruit as it grows.

✲ Keep netting over broccoli plants to protect them from birds and insects and if you have a greenhouse, check regularly for infestations of aphids.

✲ When tidying the garden, leave a section overgrown to attract hedgehogs. Piles of leaves and logs create nesting areas. Leave a small hole in fences so they can move around.

TRANSFORM YOUR GARDEN ON A BUDGET

June
ABUNDANCE IN THE GARDEN

June is a glorious month with beds and borders taking centre stage. It's also a busy time for sowing and planting, with harvesting to look forward to!

Star of the month

FOXGLOVE (*DIGITALIS*)
It's foxglove season, and spires of bell-flowers that are adored by bumble bees dominate this month. Try 'Firebird' (shown), which produces coppery pink flowers.
H1.8m

GARDENING CALENDAR

5 ESSENTIAL JOBS

1 Water succulents and cacti when the compost is dry. Place houseplants outside for a summer holiday.

2 Now that slugs and snails are about go on a torch-lit hunt treat vulnerable young plants with Nemaslug – the effects will last for six weeks.

3 Drape netting over blueberries, currants and cherries to keep birds off; protect strawberries too.

4 Deadhead perennials such as catmint, geum, astrantia and scabious before seed sets to encourage a second flush.

5 Give tomato plants in the greenhouse a shake to help pollination and ensure a good crop. Pinch out the side-shoots of single-stemmed cordon toms.

Seasonal container

Try a regal-looking purple container including a soft mix of *Lavender stoechas*, purple-blue flowering pansies and *Helichrysum petiolare* 'Silver' to trail the sides. Feed fortnightly with a high-potash liquid feed such as Tomorite to keep your display blooming throughout the month. Both butterflies and bees will love the lavender scents, and if you place it in a high-traffic area of the garden, so will you and your guests!

BEDS & BORDERS

✻ It's around now that you will see any obvious gaps in borders. Fill with astrantia, bearded iris and hardy geraniums and the bees will thank you. ✻ As well as planting, a daily potter to deadhead, tie in stems and pull weeds is therapeutic. ✻ Forget-me-nots can be cleared, but bulb foliage must be left for six weeks. ✻ Stake top-heavy perennials in case of strong winds and water borders thoroughly once a week.

What to do in the ... VEG PATCH

✻ Now is the optimum time for starting beetroot, annual spinach, radish and a wide selection of salad leaves, and herbs such as basil, coriander or parsley. Sow in succession every two weeks into pots before transplanting outdoors to guarantee a continuous crop.

✻ Carrot fly is a nuisance in summer, so choose varieties ideal for pots or raised troughs as they will bring the crop above the flying level of this pest. Choose the round 'Parmex', 'Atlas' or slim-rooting 'Amsterdam Forcing' (pictured right).

✻ Lift autumn-sown carrots, early potatoes (ready for harvesting when the flowers open), autumn-sown onions and pick salad leaves, peas, broad beans, brassicas, leafy greens and the first outdoor courgettes.

Wildlife watch

✻ The Wildlife Trust's '30 Days Wild' encourages us to pledge to do one thing for wildlife each day of June. This activity will help you and your family get close to nature. Ideas include sowing wildflower seeds in a sunny patch or container; creating a log pile for beetles and other insects; erecting a bee hotel; providing access for hedgehogs through your fence; and identifying a wildflower and finding out what wildlife it attracts.

FEATURE WENDY HUMPHRIES PHOTOGRAPHS ALAMY STOCK PHOTO, FUTURECONTENTHUB.COM

TRANSFORM YOUR GARDEN ON A BUDGET | 123

July
CUTTING AND HARVESTING

Summer is in full swing as gardens burst with blooms and fruit and veg is ripe for picking. Perk up bedding and border plants with a good watering and feed

5 ESSENTIAL JOBS

1 Mow the lawn just once a fortnight to keep it healthy during dry periods – taller leaves develop longer roots which can withstand drought, leaving you time to relax and enjoy the garden.

2 Save water by not irrigating a dry, yellowing lawn. It will soon green up again when the rain returns.

3 Plant autumn-flowering bulbs, such as colchicums and nerines.

4 Most trees should be pruned in winter, but cherries, plums and damsons are best trimmed in the summer to prevent silver leaf disease.

5 Cut back the whippy stems of wisterias to within five or six buds of the main stems – they will need another, more drastic, cut in winter too, to keep them looking healthy.

BEDS & BORDERS

✻ July isn't ideal for planting, especially if you're going on holiday and will be unable to water them. But if you do, consider installing an automatic watering system. ✻ Add a mulch of compost or shredded bark over damp soil after rain to trap moisture. ✻ Deadhead perennials, such as dahlias, hardy geraniums and salvias, and annual bedding plants, to prolong the show. ✻ Remove faded flowers on hebes, buddleias and repeat-flowering roses, taking the stems down to a healthy bud or side stem.

Star of the month
SALVIA NEMOROSA
This perennial will complete your July border with slender stems of vivid blue-purple flowers, loved by bees. It will bloom until autumn in full sun or dappled shade. H50cm

Wildlife watch

✻ Bees and butterflies will be out in force, so provide nectar-rich plants. *Verbena bonariensis*, buddleia, lavender and sage, along with marigolds and snapdragons, will top up supplies. Night-scented plants, such as tobacco (*Nicotiana*) and evening primrose (*Oenothera biennis*) attract moths, which in turn feed bats.

✻ If slugs and snails are eating your plants, replace them with more bullet-proof species. Snails love hostas, but rarely touch ferns, which will look equally beautiful in shady spots.

124 | TRANSFORM YOUR GARDEN ON A BUDGET

GARDENING CALENDAR

August
SUMMER AT ITS BEST

A busy month, maintenance is key. Snip off dead heads to keep flowers blooming, trim off any faded foliage and keep up fortnightly liquid feeds

Star of the month
DAHLIA 'TROPICAL BREEZE'
Showy dahlias are the stars of the cutting garden from midsummer to late autumn. Eye-catching 'Tropical Breeze' blooms from late May to October. **H45cm**

Wildlife watch
* Ponds and water features play an important role for wildlife in your garden. A layer of gravel or flat stones creates a perfect habitat for wildlife to cool off in the August heat. It also allows birds, hedgehogs and insects such as honeybees and hornets to drink without risk of drowning.
* Top up with rainwater from a water butt rather than tap water.

BEDS & BORDERS
* Water evergreen shrubs like rhododendrons and camellias thoroughly this month to make sure that next year's buds develop well. * Prune all summer flowering shrubs such as climbing hydrangeas as soon as they have finished flowering. * After wisteria has finished flowering remove the whippy side shoots, leaving about 20cm remaining. * It's time to plant late-flowering clematis for a colour boost.

5 ESSENTIAL JOBS

1 Keep plants and pots watered well. Water in the early morning, aiming the hose at the roots.

2 Give lavender bushes a trim as soon as they finish flowering, trimming away old flowering spikes and the top 2-3cm of leaves. Don't cut back into older wood as the flowers will grow from this next year.

3 Collect seedheads once the seedheads or pods have ripened and are dry and brittle. Gather them on a dry day, ideally after a rain-free spell, so they don't go mouldy.

4 Deadhead plants and flowers as soon as they start to fade to encourage more blooms.

5 Take cuttings of tender perennials such as pelargoniums before you store them over winter.

FEATURE GERALDINE SWEENEY PHOTOGRAPHS ALAMY STOCK PHOTO

TRANSFORM YOUR GARDEN ON A BUDGET | 125

September
TRANSITIONING TO AUTUMN

This is the time to get the garden ready for the months ahead – by collecting seed, sowing hardy annuals and winter veg, and keeping on top of falling leaves

Wildlife watch

✶ September is traditionally a time to start tidying the garden but if you're trying to encourage wildlife, don't go too far.

✶ By all means rake up fallen leaves (store in pierced bags to make leaf mould) but leave some piles to provide habitat for insects and hedgehogs.

✶ Similarly, leaving the skeletons of perennials and grasses standing over winter means that birds can feed on the seedheads and that spiders – voracious eaters of garden pests – have plenty of choices of where to spin their webs.

Star of the month
ANEMONE HUPEHENSIS VAR. JAPONICA 'SPLENDENS'
A beautiful Japanese anemone with striking, deep rose-coloured flowers which bloom for several weeks. Does well in sun or part-shade. H80cm

BEDS & BORDERS

✶ September is the best month to think about seeds – both harvesting it from plants (choose a dry day) and sowing the seeds of hardy annuals such as nigella, ammi and cornflowers, giving them time to develop a sturdy root system before spring. ✶ It's also a good time to divide congested summer-flowering perennials – plants that look too big for their spot or a bit bare in the centre. Lift and either pull gently apart or, if the roots are tangled, cut or saw down the middle. Then simply replant the sections with a little garden compost, or pot up and overwinter in a frost-free environment to bulk up.

5 ESSENTIAL JOBS

1 Show your lawn some TLC. Rake it thoroughly with a wire rake to remove moss and thatch, then spike it to aerate the soil and improve drainage. A sprinkling of phosphate feed wouldn't go amiss either.

2 Ponds need attention too – clear any duckweed or algae, cut back overhanging plants and net the surface to stop leaves falling in and suffocating your fish.

3 Trim and mulch hedges (when the soil is damp, to conserve moisture).

4 Plant alliums, crocuses and daffodils – but not yet tulips – ready for spring.

5 Order winter bedding plugs such as cyclamen and primula from catalogues or online nurseries and plant them out when they arrive.

GARDENING CALENDAR

October
AUTUMN IS HERE

The days are shorter and there is a chill in the air. It's a time when the leaves begin their glorious show of colour, making it one of the most stunning times in the garden

5 ESSENTIAL JOBS

1 After flowering, prune climbing and rambling roses and tie in stems to prevent any breakages in extreme weather.

2 Mow lawns before the weather gets too wet and cold, re-seed bare sections or re-turf. It's also a good time to aerate the grass by using a garden fork as waterlogging can be common over winter.

3 Empty out old pots and tomato plants from your greenhouse and give them a good clean to help tackle any pests and diseases over winter.

4 As leaves begin to fall, regularly sweep up. Use leaves to make leafmould, which once well rotted, can be used as compost.

5 Cut back the fruited canes of raspberries to the ground and tie in the new green canes with wire ready for next year.

Star of the month
PYRACANTHA
This spiny evergreen shrub comes alive with bright berries, standing out against greenery this month. You'll find blackbirds feasting on them.
H2.5m

BEDS & BORDERS

✷ After flowering, perennials can be cut back in autumn to help improve flowering the following year, although do leave some so wildlife have food over the winter months. ✷ Collect and store seed from seedheads to grow next year. Divide plants as needed and give them a good mulch to help protect plants over winter and to suppress weeds. Bark chips, well rotted manure or leafmould are all good to use. ✷ For healthy dahlias next year, lift the plants after the first frosts, cutting back the stems. Rinse off the soil from the tubers and pack into a pot with dry compost before storing in a dry shed.

Wildlife watch

✷ If you've planted spring bulbs, cover the pots with netting to stop squirrels digging them up. Prevent black spot from forming on roses over winter by clearing away fallen rose leaves.

✷ Clean bird feeders regularly, especially after a downpour, to stop the food from turning mouldy and keep them topped up. Make sure bird baths are also cleaned and refilled regularly.

✷ Leaving some seedheads provides shelter for insects over autumn and winter.

✷ Provide food for hedgehogs to help fatten them up in the run-up to hibernation. If you see a hedgehog during daylight hours call your local rescue for advice as it may be ill.

TRANSFORM YOUR GARDEN ON A BUDGET | 127

November
PREPARE FOR NEXT YEAR

It's all about protecting plants this month, checking tree ties and tying in shoots on plants to prevent any damage occurring from the harsh winter weather

5 ESSENTIAL JOBS

1 Continue to stay on top of fallen leaves by collecting regularly.

2 Cut back on watering houseplants so often as the temperatures drop.

3 Make a plan for next year, deciding on any planting that is needed and order plants and seeds well in advance. Decide what to grow in the veg garden and plan your beds accordingly.

4 If there is a dry spell, water pots and make sure they are lifted off the ground so they don't get waterlogged during winter.

5 Give garden tools a clean and sharpen.

Star of the month
CORNUS SANGUINEA 'MIDWINTER FIRE'
Dogwoods such as *Cornus sanguinea* 'Midwinter Fire' really stand out, having shed their mid-green leaves and leaving the fiery stems for winter interest. H2m

BEDS & BORDERS

✻ Planting wallflowers will give a border a bright burst of colour when many other plants have finished flowering. ✻ If you need holly with berries for your Christmas decs, now is the time to collect it before the birds feast on all the berries. ✻ Clear borders of leaves and fallen branches. Continue to weed beds and mulch if you haven't already. ✻ Plant bare root roses to give them time to establish.

Wildlife watch
✻ **Continue to feed birds with a high-fat diet of suet-based products and rich seeds.**

✻ **Choose plants for the garden which produce berries in winter to provide a natural source of food for wildlife.**

128 | TRANSFORM YOUR GARDEN ON A BUDGET

GARDENING CALENDAR

December

MIDWINTER MAGIC...

The days are short but filled with winter sunshine. It's a forager's delight when it comes to natural decorations – berries, twigs and seedheads take centre stage

Wildlife watch

* Wash bird feeders with soapy water, then keep them topped up with a mix of seeds, nuts and grains. In wet winters remove any soggy bird food as it can quickly rot.
* Make sure feeders are located in a sheltered position.
* Build a log pile in the garden too, as birds like wrens enjoy foraging in them for insects.
* When it's freezing place a small ball in your bird bath to give birds easy access to unfrozen water.

Star of the month

EVERGREEN COTONEASTER
The evergreen shrub *Cotoneaster lacteus* will look good all year round. Large clusters of small white flowers are followed by small red berries in autumn and winter. H90cm

BEDS & BORDERS

* Winter is the time to prune climbing roses. If you don't, you will end up with masses of twiggy growth and less blooms next year. Thin out side shoots by cutting above a bud in the direction you want your rose to grow, then tie in the stems.
* You can grow flower seeds even in midwinter as long as you have a heated propagator or warm windowsill. Try sowing sweet peas indoors, using cardboard loo rolls so they can easily be transferred outside when the weather warms up. When 10cm tall pinch out the growing tips to encourage them to bush up. This variety is 'Nimbus' (above) from Sarah Raven.

5 ESSENTIAL JOBS

1 Make sure climbing plants are securely attached to their supports with ties. Check tree ties and stakes too.

2 Dig over empty borders and pile manure on top. It doesn't have to be perfect as you can leave it to the worms and frosts to break up soil.

3 Harvest holly berries for making Christmas garlands and wreaths. Stand them in a bucket of water until you need them.

4 Lift and divide established clumps of rhubarb to renew the plant and get more.

5 Keep looking after your lawn. Clear leaves off regularly to prevent dead patches.

TRANSFORM YOUR GARDEN ON A BUDGET | 129

TRANSFORM YOUR GARDEN ON A Budget

Future PLC Quay House, The Ambury, Bath, BA1 1UA

Transform Your Garden on a Budget Editorial
Group Editor **Philippa Grafton**
Senior Art Editor **Stephen Williams**
Head of Art & Design **Greg Whitaker**
Editorial Director **Jon White**
Managing Director **Grainne McKenna**

Style at Home Editorial
Editor **Lisa Fazzani**
Art Editor **Lara Evans**
Content Director **Laura Crombie**
Group Art Editor **Alison Walter**

Cover images
Alamy

Photography
All copyrights and trademarks are recognised and respected

Advertising
Media packs are available on request
Commercial Director **Clare Dove**

International
Head of Print Licensing **Rachel Shaw**
licensing@futurenet.com
www.futurecontenthub.com

Circulation
Head of Newstrade **Tim Mathers**

Production
Head of Production **Mark Constance**
Production Project Manager **Matthew Eglinton**
Advertising Production Manager **Joanne Crosby**
Digital Editions Controller **Jason Hudson**
Production Managers **Keely Miller, Nola Cokely, Vivienne Calvert, Fran Twentyman**

Printed in the UK

Distributed by Marketforce – www.marketforce.co.uk
For enquiries, please email: mfcommunications@futurenet.com

Transform Your Garden on a Budget First Edition (HOB5756)
© 2024 Future Publishing Limited

We are committed to only using magazine paper which is derived from responsibly managed, certified forestry and chlorine-free manufacture. The paper in this bookazine was sourced and produced from sustainable managed forests, conforming to strict environmental and socioeconomic standards.

All contents © 2024 Future Publishing Limited or published under licence. All rights reserved. No part of this magazine may be used, stored, transmitted or reproduced in any way without the prior written permission of the publisher. Future Publishing Limited (company number 2008885) is registered in England and Wales. Registered office: Quay House, The Ambury, Bath BA1 1UA. All information contained in this publication is for information only and is, as far as we are aware, correct at the time of going to press. Future cannot accept any responsibility for errors or inaccuracies in such information. You are advised to contact manufacturers and retailers directly with regard to the price of products/services referred to in this publication. Apps and websites mentioned in this publication are not under our control. We are not responsible for their contents or any other changes or updates to them. This magazine is fully independent and not affiliated in any way with the companies mentioned herein.

FUTURE Connectors. Creators. Experience Makers.

Future plc is a public company quoted on the London Stock Exchange (symbol: FUTR)
www.futureplc.com

Chief Executive Officer **Jon Steinberg**
Non-Executive Chairman **Richard Huntingford**
Chief Financial and Strategy Officer **Penny Ladkin-Brand**

Tel +44 (0)1225 442 244

Part of the
Style at Home
bookazine series